PUTTING
The Stroke-Saver's Guide

Sports Illustrated Winner's Circle Books

BOOKS ON TEAM SPORTS

Baseball
Basketball
Football: Winning Defense
Football: Winning Offense
Hockey
Lacrosse
Pitching
Soccer

BOOKS ON INDIVIDUAL SPORTS

Bowling
Competitive Swimming
Cross-Country Skiing
Figure Skating
Golf
Putting
Racquetball
Running for Women
Skiing
Tennis
Track: Championship Running
Track: The Field Events

SPECIAL BOOKS

Backpacking
Canoeing
Fly Fishing
Mountain Biking
Scuba Diving
Small-Boat Sailing
Strength Training
Training with Weights

PUTTING

The Stroke-Saver's Guide

by John Garrity

Photography by Bill Jaspersohn

Sports Illustrated
Winner's Circle Books
New York

Photo credits: Heinz Kluetmeier, pp. 3, 25, 52, 106-107, 108; Michael O'Bryan, p. 10; John Iacono, pp. 13, 36; James Drake, p. 22; Paul Kennedy, p. 24; Jacqueline Duvoisin, pp. 28, 58, 60, 70, 92, 100, 120; Richard Mackson, p. 78; Floyd Bright, p. 116. The caption on pages 106-107, along with the accompanying photographs, originally appeared in a slightly different form in *Sports Illustrated Golf: Play Like a Pro*, by Mark Mulvoy, copyright ©1988 by Time Incorporated. All rights reserved. All other photographs by Bill Jaspersohn.

Special thanks to Fred Harkness at Jonathan's Landing, Jupiter, Florida for his many contributions to this book.

FIRST EDITION

Designer: Kim Llewellyn

Library of Congress Cataloging-in-Publication Data

Garrity, John.
  Sports illustrated putting: the stroke-saver's guide / by John Garrity; photography by Bill Jaspersohn.

      p. cm. —(Sports illustrated winner's circle books)
    1. Putting (Golf) I. Sports illustrated (Time, inc.) II. Title.
GV979.P8G35   1991   796.352'35—dc20
ISBN 0-452-26727-7

Contents

*Love and putting are mysteries for
the philosophers to solve.
Both subjects are beyond golfers.*

—Tommy Armour

Introduction

You are the world's worst putter.

You know it. I know it. You proved it last Saturday when you yanked that sidehill 2-footer so badly that it didn't even touch the hole.

You confirm it every time you step on a golf course. You miss 3-foot putts as often as you make them. You leave 20-footers 10 feet short. ("No guts, no glory"—aren't you sick of hearing that?) You knock other putts so far past the hole that sometimes you have a bunker shot coming back.

In fact, you are pretty much incompetent anywhere around a golf green, be it from the fringe, the bunkers, or the last few yards of fairway. You use up half the shots in your round within shot-put range of the hole. You foozle chips, botch pitches, and take two or three swings to escape sand.

There are two possible reasons for this. One, you are a beginner. Or two, you should be.

It's a truism among golf professionals that weekend golfers ignore the one area of their game that needs the most work: the short game, particularly putting. The only time most of us practice putting is just before we tee off, and then we're so anxious about our first tee ball that we hardly pay attention.

What's worse, most of us have never learned to putt properly in the first place. Lacking sound fundamentals—or even a clue as to what putting technique we wish to employ—we try one quick fix after another. Pro A says, "Guide the putter blade down the target line on the follow-through." We try it, and it works! For about a half hour. Then we start pushing all our putts to the right. Pro B says, "Let the putter blade open and close naturally, like a door." We try it, and it works! For about ten minutes. Then we start hooking our putts like a field goal kicker with the yips.

11

Good putting begins with sound, consistent fundamentals.

The best advice you'll get in this book is this: *Find a technique, learn it once, and stick to it.* Any technique, applied consistently, will outperform what you're doing now—putting with your wrists today, your shoulders tomorrow, and your legs and elbows when you get really desperate. Good putting is a matter of feel, and you can't develop feel if you keep changing your technique.

Follow this advice and you will no longer be the world's worst putter. You might even become very, very good.

YOU HAVE A CHOICE

You want to learn the right way to putt, but guess what? There *isn't* a right way to putt. As Sam Snead said, "Putting is one phase of the game of golf in which the individual is permitted to indulge himself in freak ideas."

You already know this intuitively. You've seen enough golf on television to know that Arnold Palmer crouches over the ball and George Archer stands tall. Jack Nicklaus putts with his right elbow sticking out, Paul Azinger pops the ball with a short, firm stroke, and Tom Kite sometimes putts cross-handed. Betsy King kneels and aims the putter blade at her target before she stands up to address the ball. Roger Maltbie has tried putting left-handed on short putts and right-handed on long putts. Bernhard Langer grips his putter with the shaft running up his left forearm, his right hand clutching both the putter grip and his left arm. In his later years, Sam Snead putted croquet-style, facing the hole, until that technique was banned by the United States Golf Association.

Obviously you have some choices to make. You can be a "pop" putter or a "stroke" putter; you can make your hands dominant or passive; you can stand with the ball very close to your feet or not so close; you can take the putter straight back like a pendulum or let the clubface open and close during the stroke. This book will describe the various putting techniques and will help you decide which is right for you.

This book also includes chapters on chipping, pitching, and bunker play. It does *not* include shots like the knock-down wedge or the feathered 7-iron. These sophisticated strokes are variations of the full swing, covered at length in Mark Mulvoy's *Sports Illustrated Golf: Play Like a Pro.* The only full-swing shots described here are those one might encounter from about 40 yards out and closer. At this range, you can see both the pin and the contours of the green, allowing you to play the shot with your first putt in mind. Anything longer and you're really just aiming for an area of the green or trying to hit the green itself.

Some readers may wonder why the putting chapters come first, when golf

Jack Nicklaus's putting style, with the right elbow pointing almost as far outward as the left, is one of many to choose from.

is obviously played from tee to green, with the putting last. Two reasons: First, one of the greenside shots—the chip—is based on the putting stroke. It makes sense, therefore, to teach the putting stroke first. Second, most greenside shots require that you "read" the green as you would for a putt, allowing for break, grain, and other factors. This ability is fundamental to putting and is thus covered in the putting chapters.

One last piece of advice before we slip into the golf shop and start looking at putters. Don't make a chore out of the exercises in this book. Golf is a game. It is meant to be *played*. Enjoy.

PART ONE

On the Green

Which of these putters is right for you? It depends on who you are and where you play most of your golf.

1

Equipment

The best way to learn to putt is with a borrowed putter. If you can't borrow one, buy one at a thrift store or make one out of old coat hangers.

I'm being facetious, but not very. An accomplished pianist about to embark on the study of guitar will rent a guitar or buy an inexpensive model. Until he is conversant with the basic instrument, he has no way of judging the quality or appropriateness of a more expensive model.

The same holds true for a relatively simple tool like a putter. If you haven't yet learned the fundamentals of putting, you have no way of making an intelligent comparison between putter A and putter B. Not to mention putters C through Z.

And make no mistake about it, you have a whole alphabet of putters to choose from: putters of varying weights, lies, lofts, thicknesses, shapes, configurations, and alloys. There are putter heads fashioned from wood, steel, aluminum, ceramic, and stone. There are shafts of wood, steel, graphite, fiberglass, titanium, and plastic. There are old-fashioned putters that look like poorly made canes and high-tech putters that look like struts from a space module. Jack Nicklaus won the 1986 Masters with a putter that looked like a vacuum cleaner attachment. How do you sort through the options?

TYPES OF PUTTERS

Fortunately, most putters fit into one of two basic categories: blade putters and center-shafted putters. If the shaft meets one end of the clubhead, you've got a blade putter. If the blade extends in both directions from the shaft, it's center-shafted.

The blade putter is the oldest dedicated putting tool in golf. The Scots invented it a couple of centuries ago, when feather-stuffed balls were still in use and greens were as rough as cobblestone streets. In its purest form, the blade putter is the equivalent of a $\frac{1}{2}$-iron—that is, a conventional iron with a loft of about 3 degrees. In the 20th century, the blade has been compressed—made shallower, thicker, and heavier—but it's still a blade putter if the shaft and clubhead meet end to end. The upright lie of the traditional blade putter dictates a vertical putting stroke, which is why Arnold Palmer and others who favor the blade bend their bodies so far over the ball.

The center-shafted putter made its first appearance around 1900, when A. W. Knight invented the aluminum-headed "Schenectady Putter." Walter Travis used a Schenectady putter to win the 1904 British Amateur, but the device was banned in 1908 because its croquet-style straddle-the-line concept annoyed the rules makers of the Royal and Ancient Golf Club of St. Andrews, the governing body of golf outside the Americas.

Center-shafted putters returned to favor in the 1950s, when conventional putt-from-the-side models were introduced. The original Bulls-Eye putter, popularized by Acushnet, had a thin, low-profile bronze head accented with French curves. The Bulls-Eye's shallower lie allowed the golfer to putt with his arms and hands closer to his body, aiding stability. In addition, having the shaft meet the center of the blade reduced twisting on off-center hits, thus enlarging the so-called sweet spot.

The putter's sweet spot was made larger still when Karsten Solheim invented his Ping putter in 1959. (The name comes from the sound the putter makes when striking a ball.) Borrowing an innovative process called "investment casting" from the aeronautics industry, Solheim devised a center-shafted putter with a double-sided, center-cavity putter head. Later models employed perimeter-weighted heads and offset hosels (the socket into which the shaft of a club is fitted), making the Ping-style putter more forgiving on mishits.

Putters can also be categorized by head type, the three most popular styles being the *straight blade,* the *flange blade,* and the *mallet.*

The straight blade is a thin, lightweight clubhead useful for putting on fast greens, where it doesn't take much mass to get the ball rolling (example: the Bulls-Eye putter). The straight blade has the smallest sweet spot among modern putters, but some good golfers consider this an advantage. When faced with a slippery downhill putt, they intentionally hit the ball out on the toe or on some other "dead" spot on the blade.

The flange blade is the basic straight blade with a somewhat massive extension added to the back of the clubhead (example: the Ping Anser). This

From left to right: a classic blade putter; a modern mallet head; a flange putter with an offset hosel; a center-shafted straight blade.

flange is often hollowed out in spots. The cavities allow the designer to put more weight at the bottom of the head and around the perimeter, thereby enlarging the sweet spot. As a result, the ball tends to roll about the same distance whether hit on the toe, the heel, or dead center. In recent years, most tournament players have followed the examples of Jack Nicklaus and Arnold Palmer and putted with flange blades.

The third basic putter style is the mallet head, made popular in the 1950s and '60s by players like Bob Rosburg, Cary Middlecoff, and Billy Casper. The shaft of the classic mallet joins the near end of the clubhead at a steep angle—like a blade putter—but the head is heavier and shaped like a half moon (example: the Zebra). The low profile, aerodynamic shape, and head density make the mallet the ideal putter for windy conditions and/or slow greens, where you need to get the ball rolling without a lengthy backswing. It is a favorite with bold putters who bang their putts at the hole with a hammer-like stroke . . . and with bad iron players who face a lot of 50-foot putts.

The giant flange blade on the left works well on fast greens and is easy to aim on short putts. The mallet-head putter on the right is a better choice for slow greens, high winds, and long putts. Because of its rounded back it is harder to aim on short putts.

SELECTING A PUTTER

If the greens on which you play most of your golf tend to be lightning fast, the straight blade is probably your best choice. If you play a lot of different courses in different parts of the country, you'll probably be happier with a putter that's equally good on fast and slow greens—the flange blade. If you encounter mostly slow, bumpy greens, or huge greens that call for numerous long putts, you may get your best results from a mallet-head putter.

Look for a putter that you can aim with confidence. Depending on how you address the ball, some putters deceive the eye. Others are as easy to aim as a rifle with a scope. (Many, in fact, have cross hairs and alignment lines to help you.)

Should you buy a putter with a shaft that is offset or angled? Yes, if your putting technique favors either your left or right side. For reasons we'll go into in the next chapter, some golfers lean left or right when they putt and move their hands forward or back to compensate. If you putt with your weight equally distributed over both feet at address, you're best off buying a putter with a straight hosel.

The lie of the club (the angle between the shaft and the clubhead) is a matter of personal comfort, but make sure the club "soles" naturally (that is, the entire length of the head touches the ground) when you address the ball. You don't want the toe or the heel of the club off the ground.

If you like to putt "standing tall," you'll need a long upright putter. If you prefer to bend over the ball with your hands low, a short putter or a putter with a flat lie will serve you better. Try various lengths and lies until you find a putter that suits your setup and technique.

It probably goes without saying, but don't buy a putter unless you've tried it out first. At the very least, roll some putts to a target on the pro shop floor.

2

What Kind of Putter Will I Be?

Most golfers fall into one of two broad categories: those who putt the ball at the hole with a sharp, decisive stroke and those who roll the ball at the hole with a smooth, even stroke. Tour players used to use the terms "pop putters" and "stroke putters" to describe the two camps. Pop putters use their hands and wrists to putt. Stroke putters strive for "quiet hands"—they putt with an arms-and-shoulders motion.

Everybody is a pop putter some of the time. When faced with a tap-in—one of those less-than-2-foot putts that we're sure we can't miss—we instinctively poke the ball in the hole with an abrupt, confident jab.

Everybody is a stroke putter, too. Try making a 70-foot putt without turning your shoulders!

But most good putters strike their putts with either "active hands" (pop putters) or "passive hands" (stroke putters).

If you don't know which camp you're in, it's time you made a conscious choice. You can base this choice on any number of criteria, but the most important considerations are (1) who you are and (2) where you play.

WHERE ARE YOU?

Where you play is probably more important than who you are—no offense intended. Golf courses in the Northeast and Midwest tend to have greens seeded with fine-bladed cool-weather grasses. These grasses—collectively and not always accurately called "bent grasses"—provide a slick, smooth putting surface when mowed to a height of ¼ inch or less. Golf courses in the South

23

Arnold Palmer "popped" his putts with a short, wristy stroke, but he was the first to say his style wasn't for everyone. Note the knock-kneed, pigeon-toed stance—Palmer's way of keeping his body still during the stroke.

Tom Watson proved that an arms-and-shoulders stroke putter can putt just as aggressively as any wrist putter—even Palmer. Watson has won eight major championships with his firm-wristed technique.

If you do most of your putting in the presence of palm trees, you may benefit from a wristier stroke. Hot-weather grasses putt slower than the fine-bladed grasses of the North and East.

and desert regions, on the other hand, use Bermuda grass and other hot-weather grasses on their greens. Bermuda is strong and wiry and offers more resistance to a rolling ball.

Put simply, bent grass greens are smoother and faster than Bermuda grass greens. They tend to putt "true"—the ball will roll straight and turn smoothly. If you play most of your golf on these slick surfaces, you want a smooth, soft putting stroke, one that will get the ball rolling without a lot of skidding or bouncing. You should be a stroke putter.

If you play most of your golf on Bermuda greens, you may be better off popping your putts. Putting against the grain (the direction in which the grass grows), you need a firm, decisive blow just to get the ball to the hole. Putting across the grain, you still need to propel the ball firmly. Otherwise the grain will steer your ball off line.

Fast greens: stroke it. Slow greens: pop it.

Those of you who play in Hawaii or on California's Monterey Peninsula have something else to factor in: wind. Stroke putters suffer more in high winds. It's hard enough just to keep your balance in a howling gale; making a slow, smooth stroke is almost impossible. Pop putters have a clear advantage in the wind.

Big greens? Pop putters may have an advantage there, too. The arms-and-shoulders technique tends to break down if you take a long backswing, which is necessary on putts of 40 or 50 feet. It's harder to hit the sweet spot, and distance control tends to suffer.

Obviously your choice of putting style is more complicated if you play in a contradictory environment. Tom Watson learned his golf on the fast greens of the Kansas City Country Club, where gusty spring and autumn winds are common. His choice of a technique—he is an arms-and-shoulders putter—probably suits his temperament as much as his place of birth.

Which leads us to . . .

WHO ARE YOU?

Who you are *does* matter. If you are a calm, methodical person, the arms-and-shoulders stroke, with its smooth tempo, may suit you best. Conversely, if you are the bold, aggressive, get-it-done type, you may feel more natural popping your putts.

Are you over forty and fighting the yips—those jerks and tremors that afflict some golfers on short putts? Then you need to minimize your hand action: stroke it.

Do you cut diamonds or crack safes for a living? Then by all means, take advantage of your natural "feel": pop it.

Certain players benefit from a style that conflicts with or compensates for their personality. The best example is the tense, nervous golfer. If you tremble over short putts, tend to jab at the ball, and hit your putts consistently off line, it may be because your hands, wrists, and forearms can't perform under pressure. Prescription: forget pop putting and stroke the ball with the big muscles of your shoulders and back. You'll make more of those pressure putts.

The trend among touring pros, if you're interested, is away from the wristy pop putt and toward the smooth, no-wrists stroke. The pros tend to tighten up on those pressure putts—just like you!—and they find that the arms-and-shoulders technique prevents the hands from "breaking down" and guiding the ball away from the hole.

Still, there are many fine putters on the Tour who pop the ball with a short accelerating stroke—Paul Azinger, to name one. You can tell a pop putter by watching the clubhead: the follow-through is shorter than the backswing, giving the stroke a punchy hammer-to-nail look.

Can't decide which technique is for you? Then learn the arms-and-shoulders stroke and leave pop putting alone. The arms-and-shoulders stroke is easier to learn and you'll find that it holds up better under pressure. (It is also the foundation for the chipping techniques covered in Chapter 8.)

3

Grip and Setup

It is very important that you not skip past this chapter. You *must* learn the fundamentals of gripping the putter, or all the subsequent instruction will be of no value. The stroke you will be asked to practice won't work if you grip the club in an unorthodox way. It's not that an unorthodox grip is necessarily wrong—it's more a case of keeping the stroke as simple as possible.

One of the ways we do this is by holding the club so that the palms of our hands are roughly parallel to each other and perpendicular to the line of the putt. That's a mouthful, but it's really quite simple. The back of your left hand (if you're right-handed) should be facing where you're aiming. The back of your right hand should be facing in exactly the opposite direction.

Just to understand the principle, stand over a ball without a putter and pretend you have a balloon between your hands. Let your fingers curve around the balloon, but keep the backs of both hands "square" (perpendicular) to your target line. Now straighten your fingers. Your hands should be parallel. Press them together. If you're square, your thumbs will meet at the same time as your little fingers.

This is the proper relationship of the hands for arms-and-shoulders putting. The palms are parallel; the backs of the hands are square to your target line.

Now take your putter and let the head rest naturally on the ground, blade pointed at the target. Place the fingers of your left hand under the club, keeping the back of your hand square to the target, and place your thumb on top of the grip, pointing straight down the shaft. Add your right hand, taking care that your right thumb covers your left and also points down the shaft. The back of your right hand should be square to the line.

29

In the proper putting grip, the palms are always parallel, with the right palm facing in the direction of the target. (Note: If you're a lefty, the instructions in this and subsequent chapters should be "mirrored"—that is, think left hand when the text says right hand, and vice versa.)

Three Steps to a Neutral Grip

 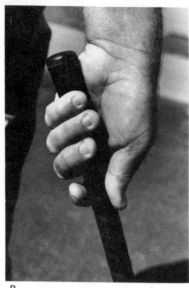 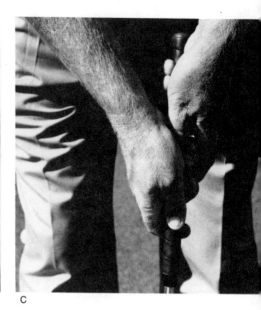

A   B   C

To achieve the neutral grip necessary to good putting, start with both palms square to the target line (A). Next, place the left hand on the club, with the thumb pointing straight down the shaft (B). Now add the right hand, with the right thumb on top of the shaft (C). Note how the base of the right thumb overlaps the tip of the left.

If you've played a lot of golf, you're probably snuggling your hands together now in what is known as the "overlapping" grip. You've raised your right pinky off the club, slid your right hand higher on the shaft, and dropped that pinky into the channel between the index and middle fingers of your left hand.

Not so fast. You can putt that way, but most good putters find that the overlapping grip permits too much independent movement of the hands. Instead, they use the "reverse overlapping" grip. Rather than lifting the right-hand pinky off the club, it's the left-hand index finger that gets lifted. And instead of letting it curl around the little finger of the opposite hand, it is straightened out and placed across the fingers of the right hand. You can think of this finger as a splint or a brace; its effect is to restrain independent hand action.

Why do we want to neutralize our hands? Because if either hand dominates the other, we tend to lose direction control.

To repeat, the basics of the putting grip are:

- hands square to the line,
- thumbs on top of the grip and pointing down the shaft,
- left forefinger extended as a brace.

Two versions of the reverse overlapping putting grip: with the left index finger curled over the right pinky (left); and with the left index finger extended across the knuckles of the right hand (right). Most good putters extend the finger to unify the hands and discourage wristiness.

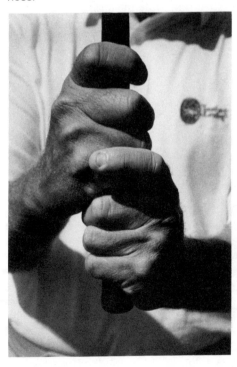 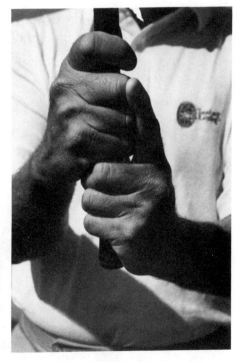

How firmly should you grip the putter? Most good putters say "firmly enough to maintain control, but not so tightly as to induce tension." If your knuckles are white, you're gripping the club way too tight. But if the putter is twisting in your hands when you hit one off-center, your grip is too weak.

GRIP VARIATION FOR WRIST PUTTERS

If you have decided that you want to putt more with your hands and wrists than with your arms and shoulders, you can allow the back of your left hand to point a little left of your target line. It is still crucial, however, that your right hand be square. The right hand is dominant in this style of putting, so most good pop putters concentrate on keeping the palm of the right hand aimed squarely down the line on which they want to start the ball rolling.

OTHER WAYS OF DOING IT

The reverse overlapping grip, while popular among fine putters, is not universal. Some good golfers putt with the regular overlapping grip, some use the interlocking grip, some use the cross-hand grip, and a few more use the baseball

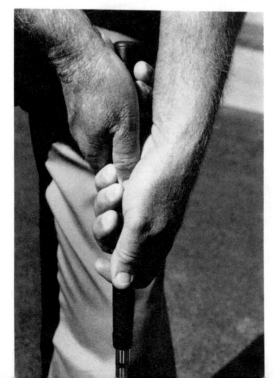

Although unorthodox, the cross-hand grip still honors the fundamentals: the right palm is aimed right down the target line.

grip, keeping all their fingers on the club. Almost without exception, though, they adhere to the fundamentals outlined above: hands square to the line, thumbs straight down the shaft. Even Bernhard Langer, with his bizarre shaft-up-the-arm style, sets up with his leading hand square to the line and his right palm facing the target.

THE SETUP

Having achieved a neutral grip, you should build a putting stance that is also as square as possible. Granted, some great players putt with their feet and hips aimed slightly left or right of the target line—Jack Nicklaus, for one—but *all* good putters set up with their shoulders square to their aim.

Keep it simple. Address the ball with your feet, hips, and shoulders square to your target line. The ball should be about an inch forward of center in your stance, allowing you to sole the putter right in the middle (opposite your breastbone). Some players like to position their hands ahead of the ball at address, but this is not recommended unless you have a putter with an offset hosel and plenty of loft. Setting up with the hands ahead delofts the putter and causes the ball to bounce or skid. (Despite its straight-faced appearance, the average putter has about 2 degrees of loft to help the ball get rolling.)

Many good putters position their hands slightly ahead of the ball at address, as shown here. This delofts the putter slightly. If your putts tend to bounce before they roll, try putting with your hands even with the ball, or switch to a putter with more loft.

Here the golfer's eyes are behind, not over, the ball. As a consequence he will tend to push his putt to the right.

With a more upright putter, the golfer can stand closer to the ball, so that his eyes are right over it, as they should be.

What's wrong with this picture? The golfer's eyes are not over the ball. He should either bend over more or switch to a more upright putter so he can stand closer to the ball.

It is critical that you feel balanced and capable of making your stroke without significant head and upper-body movement. Have someone nudge you from all sides as you stand over a putt. If you tend to topple, you need to broaden your base, lower your center of gravity, or both. Try widening your stance or flexing your knees more. In his prime, Arnold Palmer putted from a knock-kneed, pigeon-toed crouch. A hurricane couldn't have budged him.

There is one other fundamental that all good putters agree on: your eyes *must* be over the target line at address. If you set up with your head pulled back, so that your eyes are over the space between the ball and your feet, you will tend to push your putts to the right. If you set up with your eyes over the area outside the line, you will pull your putts to the left.

Some teaching pros carry a small mirror to check eye position on putts. The mirror, a few inches wide and a foot or so long, is placed behind the ball. If your eyes are directly over the line at address, you will see them in the mirror, right behind the ball.

Another method of testing eye position is to set up for a putt, pull back the putter, and then drop a ball from the bridge of your nose. If your eyes are over the line, the ball you drop should land on or right behind the ball on the ground.

4

The Putting Stroke

"There is only one mechanical secret to putting," Arnold Palmer once wrote, "and that is holding still."

Great advice. Obviously *something* has to move, but it shouldn't be your head, legs, hips, or derriere. If you putt with the arms-and-shoulders stroke, it shouldn't be your wrists, either. The arms-and-shoulders stroke is very close to the action of a pendulum. The hands do not manipulate the putter head; the wrists remain firm. As the arms take the putter back, the putter head goes inside the target line on the backswing, returns to the target line at the point of impact, and swings inside again on the follow-through. As with a pendulum, the length of the backswing and the length of the follow-through are the same. In addition, the putter is the same height off the ground at both ends of the stroke.

We say "close" to the action of a pendulum because a true pendulum swings in a perfectly vertical plane. (To achieve this, you would have to hang a center-shafted putter from your nose, which would be painful.) Instead, you make your stroke with an instrument which is several degrees off the vertical—that being the angle at which the typical putter head is joined to the shaft. This means that the club must swing inside the line going back and inside again coming through. It also means that the clubface will fan open naturally going back and close down again on the follow-through. No manipulation of the putter is necessary to accomplish this; it occurs naturally if you keep your hands still.

Try rolling a few putts along a flat section of green. Address the ball the way you learned in the last chapter: eyes over the ball, weight evenly balanced between your feet, shoulders and hips level and parallel to the target line, ball about an inch forward of center in your stance. Keeping your hands and wrists firm—no hinging, please—simply take the putter back with a one-piece move

37

The first requisite for a proper putting stroke?
Holding still.

Target line of ball

B

C

For the arms-and-shoulders stroke, the putter head goes inside the target line on the backswing (B), returns to square at impact (C, D), and swings back inside on the follow-through (E). Note how the angles between the forearms and the club remain constant throughout the stroke. Note also that the head stays down until well after impact. Lifting the head early will cause the shoulders to turn, spoiling the putt.

D   E

of your arms and shoulders. The downswing and the follow-through should be smooth and rhythmic, the wrists staying firm throughout. Don't hit the ball; stroke it.

It is very important that you complete the stroke. Many of us have a tendency, born of fear, to decelerate into the ball. As a consequence, we strike it a glancing blow or hit it an unpredictable distance. To roll the ball smooth and straight, the putter must accelerate at an even pace through the ball.

One way to achieve this is to strive for a symmetrical stroke. A 4-inch backswing gets a 4-inch follow-through; a 20-inch backswing gets a 20-inch follow-through; and so on. Putting with a symmetrical stroke will also help you achieve distance control, as we'll see in a minute.

Front View, The Arms-and-Shoulders Stroke

A

B

C

The arms do almost all the work, with the left arm guiding the club back the appropriate distance, and the right taking the club through the moment of contact with the ball and then toward the target after impact. Throughout the stroke, the wrists remain locked.

A putter with an extra-long shaft may not ▶ be for you, but it can be a useful training device for arms-and-shoulders putting. With the butt of the club anchored to the chest, the wrists can't hinge and the hands can't get busy.

D

E

F

A

B

A putt of less than 10 feet requires a very short backswing, but the putter must still accelerate through the ball. To drill on this, sink an old golf shaft into the ground behind your ball and practice putting to the hole.

CONTROLLING DIRECTION

The whole point of the arms-and-shoulders stroke is accuracy. You want to be able to deliver the clubhead to the ball exactly as you aimed it—square to the target line every time.

The wrong way to achieve this is by manipulating the putter with the hands and wrists to keep it on the target line. The putter starts back low, but it rises naturally as the arms swing back. Don't fight it! Attempting to keep the putter square to the line and close to the ground will cause your arms to pull away from your body. That disconnection, in turn, will require a difficult readjustment on the forward stroke to keep the blade square.

The same thing holds for the follow-through. Many fine players try to make the putter go straight down the target line after impact, keeping the putter low to the ground. But the wrists have to "break down" to accomplish this, and if they break down at impact or before, the putter's face will be open and the ball will go right.

Visualize this sequence: On the backstroke, the putter face opens slightly and the putter goes inside the target line. At impact, the putter face is square

The wrists must not "break down" during the arms-and-shoulders stroke. The first two photographs exaggerate the hand action that produces a push (top) or a pull (center). The third photo (bottom) shows the locked-wrists action preferred in arms-and-shoulders putting.

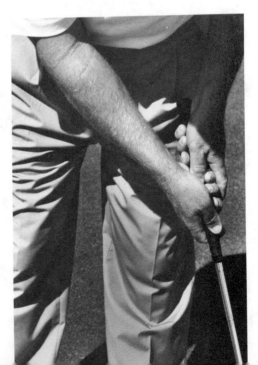

and the putter is on the target line. After impact, the putter face closes slightly and the putter winds up back inside the target line.

To ensure that you have this inside-to-inside club path, lay a two-by-four parallel to your target line and about a half inch from the toe of your putter. Then practice some putts. If you hit the board on your backswing or follow-through, you know you're going outside.

Another good way to test your accuracy: putt with a striped range ball, aligning the stripe with your target line. If you strike the ball squarely, the stripe will make a solid line on its way to the hole. Cut across the ball in either direction and the stripe will wobble like a moth in flight.

Finally, practice putting to a single hole from all directions—the classic "circle drill." Start out by placing balls in a circle about 2 feet from the hole and keep putting until you've made all the balls in the circle without a miss. Then move the balls to 3 feet, 4 feet, 5 feet, and so on. In addition to helping you groove your stroke, the circle drill will give you plenty of practice on those difficult short putts.

To practice the inside-to-inside swing path, putt with the toe of your putter a fraction of an inch from a board (left). The circle drill (right) forces you to set up and stroke the ball from different positions.

CONTROLLING DISTANCE

Professional golfers aren't much help on this subject. They've spent so many hours with the putter—literally thousands of putts a week for years on end—that they rely mostly on feel to make the ball roll a desired distance.

You can't teach feel. You can't even explain it. Who tells a basketball player how hard to launch a 20-foot jump shot? Who tells a shortstop how much juice to put on a throw to first from deep in the hole?

It's too bad feel can't be taught, because poor distance control, not bad aim, is to blame for most three-putt greens.

Think about it. From 30 feet, which putt will wind up closer to the hole? The putt that is 2 degrees off line and rolls 20 feet? Or the putt that is 12 degrees off line and rolls 32 feet?

The second putt, of course. On all but short putts, rolling the ball the right distance is more important than perfect aim. Fortunately there are ways to improve your distance control, even if you have the proverbial "touch of a blacksmith." The easiest employs a formula: *One foot equals one inch*. Take the putter back 4 inches for a 4-foot putt, 10 inches for a 10-foot putt, 20 inches for a 20-foot putt, and so on. You can practice with a yardstick laid on the ground or on a carpet. Don't worry about how far the ball actually rolls. Just practice making strokes of different lengths, taking care that the stroke is rhythmic and unhurried and that each follow-through is the same length as the backstroke.

To drill on distance control, putt with a yardstick on the green. Here a 5-foot putt gets a 5-inch backswing.

You can't take a yardstick on the golf course with you, but you *can* measure the distance from the ball to your right instep or toe. Then, when you address, say, an 8-foot putt, you will know to swing the putter back as far as your toe and no farther.

Once you've established your ability to control the length of your stroke, you can use the formula to adjust for differences in playing conditions and severity of slope. If you've got a flat 10-foot putt and you've determined that the green is slow, play it like a 15-foot putt and take a 15-inch backswing. Super-fast green? Treat your 10-foot putt like a 5-footer and make a 5-inch swing.

The same thinking applies to uphill and downhill putts. A 20-foot downhill putt won't require a 20-inch stroke — 15 inches might do, or 10, or even 5, depending on the severity of the slope and the speed of the green.

One foot equals one inch works until you're 30 feet or more from the hole. At that range, it's hard to tell how far back you're taking the putter because the clubhead is high off the ground and inside the line. What's more, really long putts call for some wrist action to get the ball to the hole.

That's why, when faced with a 40-foot putt, you might think, "Hard thirty." In other words, you'll take a 30-inch backswing and hit the ball harder than usual.

The straight-line drill will help you develop your feel for putts of varying lengths. As you move from ball to ball, your stroke should get progressively longer, but your tempo should not change. The swing for a 20-foot putt should take the same time as the swing for a 5-foot putt.

To repeat, great players don't use cut-and-dried formulas. They rely on feel. But watch them! Their strokes conform very closely to the *one foot equals one inch* formula—adjusted, of course, for the faster greens they putt on.

The numbers are arbitrary, anyway. What you're trying to do is to control distance by changing the length of your swing rather than the force of your stroke. Every stroke, no matter how long, should have the same rhythm and tempo.

Phil Mickelson, one of golf's brightest young players, has worked this principle into his pre-shot routine. Before stroking any putt, he takes three practice swings. The first swing is intentionally too long for the distance to the hole. The second is intentionally too short. The third is in between—or as Goldilocks would have it, "just right."

That's the stroke that Mickelson uses on his actual putt.

PUTTING STRATEGY: CHARGE OR LAG?

Have you given any thought to *how* you want your putts to fall in the hole?

Probably not. Sometimes you roll the ball meekly to the cup and it topples in (usually accompanied by a lot of body English from you). Other times, you hit a frozen rope that smacks the back of the cup and hops 4 inches in the air before dropping out of sight.

You'll take them any way you can get them, but the smarter strategy, on all but the shortest putts, is to let the ball topple in—what Bobby Jones called "the dying ball." A ball that is rolling slowly has a chance to fall in if it catches any part of the hole. A fast-rolling putt will drop only if it hits dead center.

Arnold Palmer won most of his tournaments by "charging" his putts, so you can't say that way is wrong. For one thing, it's a great way to straighten out those breaking putts—the fast-rolling ball is less affected by contours in the green. On the other hand, the all-or-nothing approach leaves you with a lot of lipped-out putts and long comebackers for par. The more you charge your putts, the smaller you make the hole.

The topple technique, in contrast, effectively enlarges your target—assuming, of course, that you get the ball to the hole. Try to roll the ball so that it will die a foot behind the hole if you miss. Otherwise, you'll be taken for a disciple of humorist Rex Lardner, who once defined the putter as "a club designed to hit the ball partway to the hole."

On long putts, the topple technique is called "lag putting." From 20 feet and out, you're just trying to get the ball close enough to the hole to make your next putt a gimmee. If that means leaving it a few inches short, so be it.

Don't let the "Never up, never in" crowd intimidate you. Even the top pros lag it when they're putting from long range. If they can stop the ball anywhere within 3 feet of the hole, they're happy. The ball falls in? They'll take it. But getting close *consistently* is the goal.

It's a cliche, but on long putts you should visualize a 3-foot circle around the hole and aim for that. You'll make your share of bombs without even trying.

Smart golfers "lag" the ball to the hole on long putts. Picture a circle with a 3-foot radius around the hole, and try to make your ball stop within that circle.

3 ft.

THE WRIST STROKE

In his prime, Arnold Palmer was so wristy that he barely moved his arms when putting. Billy Casper and Bob Rosburg "popped" their putts, taking a short backswing and accelerating briskly through the ball. Even Sam Snead, that paragon of smoothness and tempo, was once a committed wrist putter.

The wrist stroke obviously offers certain advantages. It is an aggressive stroke, and some players like that. It enhances "touch"—the hands being more sensitive than the arms and shoulders. It requires a shorter backswing, which offers certain advantages in setting up and aiming.

We've already discussed some of the disadvantages. Foremost among them is the wrist stroke's tendency to self-destruct when the golfer reaches a certain age. The yips have driven many a wrist putter through the doors of the arms-and-shoulders school.

The Wrist Stroke

Here the right hand does most of the work. The wrists hinge slightly on the takeaway (A), then the right hand accelerates the putter head into the ball (B). Note the short follow-through (C). The wrist putt is more of a hit or a "pop" than a sweeping action. The key is to develop a feel for the putt with the right hand.

A

B

C

Nonetheless, the wrist stroke has its adherents, and it may be right for you. Here are a few pointers:

1. The same fundamentals apply: shoulders square, hands square, eyes over the target line.

2. The ball can be played in the middle of the stance or farther forward. If you choose to play the ball up by your left foot, move your weight and your hands to the left and use a putter with an offset hosel and generous loft.

3. The backswing is short. Hinge the wrists as you take the club back. Then deliver the putter head to the ball with a dominant right hand.

4. Guide the putter down the target line as long as possible on the follow-through.

This last point is important. If you allow your wrists to break down at impact or "release," as they would in a full swing, you'll push, pull, and spin your putts all over the green. Keep your wrists firm through the ball.

To work on this, go back to doing the circle drill from 2 feet. But don't stroke the putts inside-to-inside. Pop the putts instead, keeping the clubface square to the target after impact.

THE ARMS-AND-SHOULDERS POP PUTT

PGA Tour star Paul Azinger putts brilliantly using a stroke that combines the pendulum action of the arms-and-shoulders stroke with the short backswing of the pop stroke. On a 30-foot putt, Azinger takes the putter back no farther than the outside of his right foot. On the follow-through he drives his putter straight at the hole.

"Most amateurs that I play with stroke the ball too long on the way back and then decelerate," Azinger says. "They virtually stop the putter head at the ball. It's very hard to be consistent that way."

Some would argue that it's very hard to control distance Azinger's way, but he seems to have no trouble. He contends that his "short accelerated stroke" is also more repeatable under pressure.

If you want to test Azinger's method, you can devote some practice time to his short-stroke drills. From 2 feet, he pushes the ball into the hole with no backswing at all, just a croupier's shove. When he has made twenty in a row, he repeats the drill with a backswing about an inch long. When he's made twenty straight of those, he moves back to 6 feet and putts with his normal short stroke till he's made ten straight.

Even if you don't putt Azinger's way, these drills can help you avoid the deceleration trap.

5

Reading Greens

A sound putting stroke does not guarantee good putting. You must also learn to aim correctly and to hit the ball with the proper force.

For beginning golfers this is extremely difficult. It takes hours of practice and many rounds of actual play to become a good predictor of how the ball will roll on an unfamiliar green. Every putt is different.

Or is it? There is a saying in golf: "Every putt is a straight putt." That's because you never intentionally put curve spin on a putt. You hit it straight. After that, the ball takes a path dictated by three forces of nature: gravity, wind, and friction. (Four forces, if you believe in body English.)

Gravity, if you don't have your high school physics text handy, is the force that causes a rolling ball to follow a curved path on a tilted surface. The steeper the slope, the greater the curve, all things being equal. Gravity is usually the easiest of the three forces to consider; the slope of the green is, after all, visible at a glance.

Wind is more problematic. It's invisible, it blows in gusts, and it changes direction at whim. Fortunately, the influence of the wind on putting is negligible in all but extreme weather conditions.

Friction—that's the tough one. Everything the ball touches on its roll toward the cup—grass, sand, water, spike holes, whatever—slows the ball or deflects it. The frictional force is anything but consistent, and it takes a keen mind and patience to calculate its effects.

As you approach the green from the fairway, start reading it by looking for any prevailing tilt.

PREDICTING BREAK

For the average golfer, guessing how much a putt will break is about as sophisticated as green reading gets—or ought to get. It's simply a matter of sizing up the contours of the green and deciding which way the ball will curve on its way to the hole.

Too many golfers don't start this process until they are on the green and marking their balls. This can blind them to the overall tilt of the terrain. Most good putters avoid this by paying attention to the green as they approach from 40 or 50 yards out. From this distance, the overall slope of the green emerges from the architect's camouflage of mounds and swales.

As you approach the green, look also for the functional slopes built into every green. Most modern greens are tilted back to front to make them more receptive to incoming shots. Greens also need places for rainwater to run off, and these slopes are most often at the front or sides. If you see a pond or a catch basin 30 yards to the left and below a green, that's a pretty sure sign that at least part of the green slopes in that direction. For similar reasons, it's rare to find a putt that breaks directly into a sand bunker; the architect designs the green so that runoff will not flow into the sand.

You must always be alert to the prevailing terrain. If you have mountains on the left and an ocean on the right, the prevailing terrain is downhill right. A putt that looks flat may actually break left to right. Similarly, if you're putting toward mountains, expect the ball to break away from the highest peak.

This golfer's putt will break right, toward the water. It's not magnetism—the green is sloped that way for drainage.

Once you're on the green, you should read for break quickly and efficiently. The shrewd putter hustles over and lifts the flag. That way, he can pace off the distance between the hole and his ball without delaying play.

If you are not the first to putt, study the line from two directions—from behind the ball and from behind the hole. Get as low as possible; squat if necessary. Subtle slopes are harder to read from a steep angle. Another good vantage point is midway between the ball and the hole on the low side. This view tells you whether you are putting uphill or downhill. And don't just read with your eyes—your feet can often tell you if the green is concealing a prevailing tilt.

Another common technique for judging break is the plumb bob. To plumb bob a putt, stand behind the ball and hold your putter like a pendulum, suspended between thumb and forefinger, in front of your dominant eye. With the other eye closed, line the shaft up with your ball. If the hole appears on the left side of the shaft, the ground you're standing on slopes left. If the hole appears on the right side of the shaft, it slopes right.

Some players swear by the plumb bob, but just as many think it's bunk. "It looks like something Ray Charles would do," one pro told me. "If you can't tell which way a putt breaks by looking at it, you've got problems."

When plumb bobbing, remember to sight with your dominant eye. And watch out for those double-breaking putts!

Most good putters size up the break at a glance. You should, too. In putting, your first read is usually the best read.

READING GRAIN

Predicting the effect of sloping ground on a putt—the gravity part—is easy. It's the frictional force that confounds the average golfer.

Let's restate the obvious. Golf greens are covered with grass, and grass does not emerge from the ground in rigid vertical spikes. Grass blades grow at an angle dictated by sunshine, water, and wind. This prevailing direction we refer to as *grain*.

You don't need to go outside to understand this principle. Just run your hand across a section of common cut-pile household carpet. If you rub with the grain, the carpet fibers lie flat and give the material a pale, unblemished look. Go against the grain, however, and you get a dark, roughed-up look. That's because the fibers are standing up and no longer reflect light evenly.

Grass behaves the same way. You can't see it, but most of those little blades are bending in the same direction. With closely mowed fine-bladed grasses, the influence on a rolling ball is minimal, but hot weather grasses, like Bermuda grass, tend to jostle the ball around. Downgrain putts roll fast and far, while putts into the grain decelerate or even bounce. Putts across the grain take a physicist to decipher.

Fortunately most golf courses have "prevailing grain." That is, all the grass tends to grow in the same direction, usually toward the setting sun. (On Maui, they say the grass grows in the direction of Molakai. That's a little north of the setting sun, but it's beautiful any way you look at it.) It's not a violation of the rules to ask before a round which way the grass grows, but you never hear this question when golfers gather in the pro shop. Pity.

Out on the course, the easiest way to determine grain is to drag your putter across the short fringe grass. As in the carpet example, the putter will slide smoothly with the grain. Against the grain, it will rough up and darken the grass. Unfortunately this sure-fire method of grain detection is against the rules. Employ it in practice rounds for educational purposes only.

The more accepted reading technique uses reflected light. Simply look at the grass from different angles. If the grass appears light green and glossy, the grain is away from you. If the grass appears a darker, flat green, you are staring into the teeth of the grain.

You can sometimes determine the grain by examining the edges of the

A putter dragged against the grain leaves this fringe grass looking roughed up. Stroked the other way, the grass will lie flat and smooth.

The shaggy left edge and the clean right edge of this hole reveal that the grass is growing from left to right. Can you tell from the shadow what time of day this photo was taken?

hole. If the grass has had time to grow since the hole was cut, it will be growing over the edge on one side of the cup and away from the edge on the opposite side.

Having determined the direction of the grain, simply include that information in your estimation of speed and break. Example: On a dead-flat 10-foot putt, the basic formula calls for a 10-inch stroke. Into the grain, you might pretend it's a 12-foot putt and lengthen your stroke accordingly. Downgrain, you might think "eight-footer." Downhill and downgrain, a putt can roll forever. You'll need an even shorter stroke.

Crossgrain putts don't affect the length of your stroke that much, but they can add or detract from the amount the ball breaks. You'll often hear a touring pro say, "I tried to putt it through the grain." That just means he hit the putt harder so it wouldn't slip sideways before reaching the hole. Don't try this yourself unless you're confident of your ability to make the 5-footers coming back.

The idea on crossgrain putts is simply to allow for a little more or a little less break, depending on which way the grain runs. For instance, a putt that

Pro golfers have a reason for scrutinizing a putt closely—they get paid for what they do. Lacking such an excuse you should avoid undue delays on the green.

looks as if it should be played an inch outside the hole may actually be a straight putt if the grain is working against the break. A long lag putt, on the other hand, may fall off sharply downgrain as it dies.

Finally, be alert to changing conditions. Grass continues to grow while you're playing on it, so don't be surprised if the greens putt slower in the afternoon than they did in the morning. Exception to the rule: windy days. Wind can dry greens out, making them faster.

Too Much Reading
Is Bad for the Eyes

Before we leave this subject, a cautionary note: In the golf curriculum, reading grain is graduate-level stuff. The high-handicapper who examines every inch of the green with a studious frown—like a trout fisherman searching the surface of a brook for tell-tale ripples—invites ridicule. Show respect for your playing partners and the golfers behind you by lining up your putts without undue delay or hotdogging.

6

Special Situations

Now that you have mastered the mechanics of putting and learned a thing or two about reading greens, it's time to get real. Golf is not played on a putting clock. It's played out in the elements on sometimes rugged or poorly maintained terrain. You will occasionally find the path between your ball and the hole littered with soil cores left by an aerating machine. The green may be riddled with spike holes and unrepaired ball marks. The wind may be howling. Robert Trent Jones may have buried an elephant in the green.

Good putters know how to deal with these contingencies.

PUTTING FROM THE FRINGE OR COLLAR

On most greens, the first cut of fringe grass is short enough to putt from. In deciding whether to putt or chip, you must consider the lie. The ball must be sitting up to putt. If it's nestled in a depression, take a chipping club and pop it out with a downward stroke.

You should also examine the fringe grass very carefully before deciding to roll your ball over it. Is your path smooth? Is the fringe grass uniform in height and density? How about the grain? Remember, the effect of grain is more pronounced with longer grass. Beware of the upgrain putt into 2 or 3 feet of Bermuda grass fringe.

When putting from the fringe, it is important to guard against "stabbing" the ball instead of stroking it. You must also avoid hitting the grass first. To ensure clean contact, shift your weight a little to the left and/or play the ball back slightly in your stance. Otherwise, put a normal smooth stroke on the ball.

61

Fringe lies are one of several special situations where you must decide whether to putt or to chip. Here, Jack Nicklaus makes the right decision and putts.

A good lie on a neatly clipped fringe. This shot cries to be putted, not chipped.

From long fringe grass, move your weight forward, with the ball back, and putt with a more descending blow. If you think you might hit grass before you hit the ball, chip it instead.

The difficulty with fringe putts is usually in controlling distance. Experience will teach you how much harder to hit the ball from long grass, but a good starting point is to devise some artificial formula, such as "two inches of swing for every foot of fringe." If you have 2 feet to the putting surface and 15 more to the hole, you might pretend you have a 19-foot putt instead of 17.

You will find that the more fringe you have to negotiate (as a percentage of the putt's total length), the more difficult it is to judge distance. Two feet of fringe is not that significant if you're 40 feet from the flag; 2 feet is trouble if you've only got 10 feet to the hole, all of it downhill.

As a rule, putting from the longer fringe grasses (the "second cut") is not a good idea. The lie must be ideal, you must be putting downgrain, and the ball must be right on the edge of the putting surface for this shot to work.

BALL RESTING AGAINST A GRASS COLLAR

If the ball is resting 2 or 3 inches from high grass, you can putt it. Just lean left and play the ball back in your stance. This creates a steeper angle of attack, allowing you to stroke the ball without tangling your blade in the grass. (Don't be surprised if the ball bounces a couple of times.)

If the ball is actually leaning against the collar, leave your putter in the bag. This is a shot for your sand wedge. Use your putting grip (reverse overlapping), and address the ball with the clubface square to the target line and the clubhead hovering just off the ground. Then, using a normal arms-and-shoul-

Putt with a sand wedge when your ball comes to rest against a collar. Just belly the ball with your normal arms-and-shoulders stroke.

ders putting stroke, "belly" the ball with the flange of the wedge. The sole of the wedge is heavy enough to plow through the grass, and the ball will come out like a putt.

This is not a trick shot. Practice it a few times and you'll be able to use it with confidence when the need arises.

STEEP UPHILL PUTTS

Because the ball decelerates rapidly on uphill putts, you must hit it much harder and allow for less break. Picture this as a straight putt with a little hook on the end.

Make certain, also, that your hips and shoulders are aligned more or less with the slope. Leaning left into the hill can cause you to pull the putt or "pinch" it against the grass.

STEEP DOWNHILL PUTTS

Here the ball decelerates slowly and the break is exaggerated. Take a much shorter stroke, roll the ball smoothly, and—if it's a breaking putt—allow for the ball to bend generously on its way to the hole. To avoid a long comeback putt, try to make the ball topple in.

But don't leave it short. You don't want two downhill putts in a row, like the guy on the Senior Tour who moaned, "I could putt it off a tabletop and still leave it halfway down the leg."

EXTREME SIDEHILL PUTTS

Big-breaking putts, especially the left-to-right kind, are a problem for many golfers. There is a tendency to peek at the hole and then steer the putter in that direction, causing either a pull or a push. It is important to choose a target— say, a spike mark 2 feet to the right of the hole—and then putt to that target, ignoring the hole. This requires discipline, and discipline comes with practice.

It is also important to remember that most putts don't bend like a rainbow, but break more sharply as they slow down. In other words, speed, not just aim, determines where the ball will wind up. Hit the ball too softly and it will die well short of the hole and below it. Hit it too firmly and the break won't take until the ball is well past the hole. It takes perfect speed for the ball to die into the hole.

That's why the pros refer to these as "speed putts." Watch them in practice rounds before a tournament and you'll see them rolling ball after ball from sidehill lies, testing the speed needed to hole a putt.

Another thing: if the ball is higher than your feet, stand more erect than usual and sole the putter flat on the ground before making your stroke. This way you can avoid cutting across the ball or stubbing the toe on the ground. If the ball is lower than your feet, stand closer to it and bend over more. You want to ensure that your stroke follows the contour of the green.

Finally, use your powers of visualization. To fall, any big-breaking putt has to come in the side door. Picture the ball dying near the hole and falling off into the cup from the side, not the front.

AUGUSTA NATIONAL IN APRIL: SUPERFAST GREENS

The United States Golf Association measures green speed with a device called a Stimp Meter. Sounds high-tech, but it's really just a little ramp down which the guys in blue blazers roll a ball. The Stimp Meter "reading" is simply the number of feet the ball rolls, on average. On the Stimp Meter, everyday-play greens are 6 or 7, tournament greens are 9 or 9.5, and linoleum is about 15.

The greens at the Augusta National Golf Club, site of The Masters, are about 12 the week of the tournament. At certain pin positions, if you place the ball a few feet below the cup, the ball will roll right off the green. Hord Hardin, the club's former chairman, once said, "We could make them so slick we'd have to furnish ice skates on the first tee."

The pros gripe about glassy conditions, but fast greens are in many ways easier to putt than average greens. The ball tends to roll true and to break predictably. And it's always an advantage to hit the ball with a short stroke.

There are just a few things to remember:

• On downhill putts, all you have to do is get the ball rolling. A 10-foot downhill putt may require no more than a 1-inch stroke. (A pro would say, "Just hit it a half-turn and let gravity do the rest.")

• Uphill putts are still uphill. The ball will still decelerate rapidly and break less than usual. Don't get scared and leave the ball halfway to the hole.

• Sidehill putts must be rolled very gently and aimed well above the hole. Remember, once the ball starts to break, it will roll like a downhill putt.

The most important rule is: "Keep the ball below the hole." Every approach shot, pitch, or chip should be targeted below the hole, leaving you a relatively easy uphill putt.

PUTTING FROM FAIRWAYS AND SAND: THE "TEXAS WEDGE"

As a rule, the club for greenside bunker shots is the sand wedge. But what if your ball is sitting up on wet sand, the bunker has practically no lip, and there's a lake 30 feet behind the pin?

If you're smart, you'll putt it. Just make certain that you can roll the ball over the lip and through any fringe grasses that may be in the way.

Technically, the Texas wedge stroke is your standard arms-and-shoulders putting stroke, with one difference: your weight should be more on your right side. (You don't want the putter to hit down on the ball, driving it into the sand.) This setup encourages a slight upswing and gets the ball rolling with a little topspin.

There's no law, either, that says you can't putt from the fairway. Good golfers do it all the time in Scotland, where the greens can be rock hard and steeply banked. For this shot, take a bigger swing than normal, but try to maintain a smooth, even tempo. A slight hinging of the wrists is inevitable if you've got a lot of ground to cover, but don't let your wrists break down at impact. Stroke firmly and decisively through the ball.

The "Texas wedge" is your everyday putter used creatively. From sand, shift your weight to the right, swing up slightly, and get the ball rolling with topspin. (Note: the harder the sand, the better your chances of getting up and down.)

WET GREENS

Greens that have been watered or rained on putt slower. Grass that is still wet from watering or rain putts slower still.

The real trouble comes when the turf is saturated. Then the ball tends to skid or hydroplane on surface water, making it very hard to determine when the break will take hold. The best strategy is to strike the ball firmly and allow for less break than normal. Most of that break will come as the ball dies near the hole.

How do you know if a green is saturated? Your feet will tell you ("Squish . . . squish . . ."). If water seeps out from under the soles of your shoes, you're working with a wet sponge.

PUTTING IN WIND

The problem here is not so much the influence that high wind has on the ball—although you must allow for that—but the influence it has on the golfer. Anything that affects your balance affects your ability to stroke the putter smoothly and accurately. Mishits are common in windy conditions.

For most golfers, the answer is to get low and get wide. The more you widen your stance and lower your body, the more stable you will be. Your putting stroke may feel somewhat restricted, but the tradeoff is worth it. You might also consider putting with a shorter, faster stroke.

If you putt terribly in the wind, don't overlook the possibility that your putter might be at fault. A heavy, small-headed putter works beautifully in the wind, but a big, light, cavity-back putter—the MacGregor Response, for example—catches the wind like a sail. If you can't take your putter back in a 30 mph wind without it darting off line, try another putter.

NOT QUITE TAP-INS:
THE "YIPS"

If you think putting is harder the closer you get to the hole, you're in good company. It was touring pro Dave Hill who said, "From five feet in to the hole, you're in the throw-up zone."

Three-time U.S. Open champion Hale Irwin once lost the British Open by a stroke because he whiffed a tap-in. Another time he missed a 15-incher in a Tour event.

Lanny Wadkins, angered when he missed a 4-footer for par at the 1991

Everybody misses a short putt now and then—everybody!

Masters, tried to backhand the tap-in and missed *that*. Scott Hoch missed a 24-incher for victory at the 1989 Masters. Sam Snead missed short putts so often in his brilliant career that he once said, "You know those two-foot downhill putts with a break? I'd rather see a rattlesnake."

One reason these putts are so difficult is the pressure we put on ourselves. If you're a typical weekend golfer, you will make a 3-footer for bogey four times out of five; for par, three times out of five; and for birdie about two times out of five. The more you want to make a putt—or the more you fear missing it—the harder it gets. Lee Trevino says his putter gets "as heavy as a wagon tongue" when he faces a big-money putt.

Another reason the short putts are so hard is that you can see the hole with your peripheral vision. This would seem to be an advantage, but it's not. There's a tendency to steer the ball toward the hole instead of stroking it down the line.

Let's tackle the nerves first. The best way to beat the shakes is by taking the small muscles of the hands and wrists out of play. In other words, putt with the arms and shoulders. The next step is to rid your body of tension: take a breath and exhale before pulling the trigger. Another trick is to ground the putter behind the ball and then lift it slightly before making your stroke. You have a much better chance of making a smooth pass at the ball if you don't have to lift it and drag it back at the same time.

More than anything else, confidence comes from knowing that your putter is square to your target line. You may find it easier to square the blade if your putter has a big blade or some sort of alignment gimmick, such as the Zebra putter's parallel lines.

As for the problem of peripheral vision, your first task is to aim your putter; your second task is to trust in your initial aim and block out further visual input. This isn't easy, but you have to train yourself to putt along your body line and keep the hands firm through impact.

And don't lift your head until you have completed your stroke! Many short putts are missed because the golfer tries to see the ball into the hole. The head comes up, the shoulders turn, and the putt gets yanked.

Technique aside, there are two strategies for short putts. You can: (1) roll them slowly and let them break into the cup, or (2) ram them firmly into the center of the cup, allowing for little or no break.

The second method is not for the faint of heart, for obvious reasons—if you miss, you'll have an even longer putt coming back. On the other hand, if you roll the ball firmly, you don't have to read the putt so accurately.

Anything inside 2 feet? Ram it straight in. Three feet and up? You be the judge. If your putt is straight and uphill, there's no reason to baby it. But if you read a lot of break in the putt, you're better off playing it to topple in on the high side.

Paul Runyan is credited with "Three for Speed," a drill that nicely illustrates your options. Putt three balls to the hole from a distance of 3 feet, making sure your putt has some break to it. Roll the first ball so that it just topples in on the high side. Hit the second putt firmly enough that the ball hits the liner at the back of the cup. On the third putt, pretend you're Tom Watson in his prime and try to make the ball hit the back lip and bounce in the air before going in. This drill will illustrate how speed influences break and will give you valuable practice on those knee-knockers.

Just remember: everybody misses a short putt now and then. If you can accept that fact, you won't lose your cool when *you* miss one. And you probably won't miss as many, either.

7

The Long Putter

If the preceding chapters haven't helped, try the long putter.

Desperation has driven better players than you or me to just that extreme. Orville Moody, one of the Tour's poorest putters in his prime, switched to a long putter in 1985 and became one of the top money winners on the Senior PGA Tour. Rocco Mediate, bothered by a bad back, went long in 1991 and became the first player to win a regular Tour event with one.

"Long" in this context means a putter in the 48- to 50-inch range, although some players, such as the Senior Tour's Frank Beard, have experimented with midsize models. Tall golfers may find that even so-called long putters aren't long enough. To be used effectively, the butt of the handle must comfortably reach the player's sternum.

The principle behind the long putter goes back to the pendulum idea, discussed in Chapter 4. Instead of suspending a putter from his nose, the golfer, standing erect, uses his left hand to anchor the butt of the club to his chest. His right hand, held much lower on the club, is used to draw the clubhead back and then guide it through the ball.

This stroke, which is primarily a shoulder motion, effectively neutralizes the hands and wrists, and that's why the long putter is so often cited as a miracle cure for the yips. In addition, the golfer's tall posture at address makes it easy to look down the target line without the distortions of perspective that attend a bent-over stance.

Sound easy? Golf purists say it's *too* easy.

"I personally think that it's not a stroke of golf, the long putt," says Tom Watson, who has won eight major championships with the short kind. "The reason I think it's not a stroke of golf is that you can literally take the putter back and just let it swing, and by its own momentum the putter will go through

Rocco Mediate was the first player to win a regular
PGA Tour event using a long putter.

the impact area. You just let the weight of the putter head carry the ball through. I don't think that's fair or right."

Having read that, you're probably ready to jump in the car and head for Nevada Bob's to buy one. But hold on. Most golfers who try the long putter find that the miracles come only with hours of dedicated practice. What's more, there seems to be a consensus that the long putter's benefits vanish on—get this—long putts. Players who rely on feel to control distance find that feel is hard to come by when you have 4 feet of plumbing jammed against your chest.

For these reasons, the long putter is still primarily a club of last resort for seniors, players with bad backs, and golfers who putt so badly that they'll try anything.

GRIP AND SETUP

The long putter is still relatively new, so there is no established dogma to dictate how you use it. Australia's Peter Senior anchors the club with his chin, while American Mark Lye steadies the shaft with his abdomen. Most players keep the club centered on their bodies, but a few move the ball closer to the left foot and let the shaft run up the side, almost to the left ear. Some, like Mediate, grip the club conventionally with the right hand, while others hold the shaft between two fingers of the upturned right hand in a grip known as the "claw."

Eccentricities aside, here is the basic grip and setup: (1) Seize the top of the shaft with your left hand as you would a microphone, elbow out. (2) Grip the middle of the club with your right hand—or claw—keeping your palm aimed down the target line. (3) Sole the putter behind the ball and pull the butt of the club to your chest so that the back of your left thumb rests against your sternum.

As always when putting, your shoulders should be square to the target line and your eyes should be over the ball. Your posture should be erect enough that you feel no strain, but not ramrod straight. Balance is as important with the long putter as with the short putter—more so, really, since the long shaft magnifies any upper body movement.

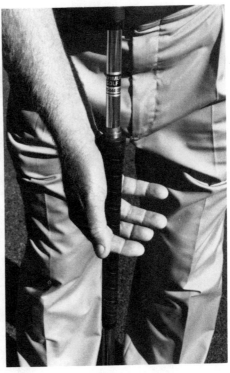

A typical long-putter stance. Some players draw either the left or right foot back, but the fundamentals still apply—the shoulders must be parallel to the target line.

The "claw." Note that the palm directly faces the target line.

THE STROKE

There are two strokes, actually. The pendulum stroke, which employs very little shoulder turn, is made by taking the club back with the right hand and more or less "releasing" it into the ball. This is the pure pendulum approach frowned upon by Watson, but it is not as easy to pull off as one might imagine. Unless your setup and posture are perfect, the clubhead tends to drift on the backswing and impart spin to the ball at impact.

The second method, a close cousin of the arms-and-shoulders stroke, calls

Here the golfer can read the break and is perfectly positioned to try to make the putt. Note especially his eye position: directly over the ball.

for a pronounced shoulder turn, with everything else frozen from the address position.

Whichever stroke you employ, you must resist the temptation to guide the putter with the right hand. It's gravity's job, not yours, to square the putter face.

The remaining chapters are devoted to the various greenside strokes: the chips, pitches, and sand escapes. To play these shots successfully you need both sound technique and skill at reading greens.

You also need a strategic sense. That is, you need to make each stroke count toward your management of the golf course. You must avoid the "no-brainers"—those foozled chips and wasted pitches that cause you to look at the sky and moan, "What was I thinking about?"

To that end, here is a greenside mantra that you should memorize or have stenciled on your golf bag:

> *If I'm close enough to see the contours of the green, I will play the shot with my first putt in mind.*
> *If I'm close enough to read the break — why not try to make it?*

PART TWO

Around the Green

8

Chipping

The chip shot is probably the easiest shot in golf, as well as the greatest stroke saver. The basic technique can be mastered in about five minutes, and occasional practice is all it takes to stay sharp.

Why, then, do so many golfers stub their chips or hit hot grounders across the greens?

The reason may lie in our tendency to distrust the club. In a misguided effort to get the ball a foot or two in the air, we lean away from the target and try to scoop the ball onto the green. This method doesn't work, but we keep trying.

Let's look at the problem. The chip shot is a micro-shot aimed at the flag with a more-or-less lofted club from a distance of 15 to 100 feet. It is struck from fairway grass or from the fringe bordering the putting surface. The swing is extremely short—no farther back than 7 o'clock, in most instances, and with practically no follow-through—and the ball flies the minimum distance necessary to get safely on the green. The rest of the trip is roll. (The chip should not be confused with the pitch, a shot that employs more body turn to hit the ball farther or higher.)

In the putting chapters, we dwelt at some length on the distinction between the wrist stroke and the arms-and-shoulders stroke. The same two approaches apply to chipping, which is why mastery of one or the other of the putting strokes makes chipping a breeze.

The difference is terminology. Teaching pros today use the terms "one-lever" and "two-lever" to describe the two chipping styles. The one-lever chip is our old friend the arms-and-shoulders stroke. The two-lever chip is a close cousin to the pop putt. (The second lever refers to the wrists, which hinge during the stroke.) Good chipping can be achieved using either method exclu-

79

With this famous chip, Tom Watson won the 1982
U.S. Open at Pebble Beach and a place in the records
for fantastic finishes.

sively, but many players learn to play both, choosing one or the other depending on the lie and other variables.

THE ONE-LEVER CHIP

The only difference between the one-lever chip and the arms-and-shoulders putting stroke is the setup. Even the grip is the same: the reverse overlap putting grip with both thumbs pointed down the shaft. Just be sure to choke up significantly on the club—some pros slide the fingers of the right hand all the way down to the bare shaft.

To hit the one-lever chip from level ground, select a lofted iron and set its leading edge behind the ball, square to the target line. Address the ball with your feet slightly open to the line and less than shoulders width apart. The ball should be back in your stance—no farther forward than center if the ball is sitting up nicely, more toward your right foot if it is nestled down in the grass. Your hands should be ahead of the ball, delofting the club. Most good chippers position their hands about even with the left thigh.

Having aimed the club and established the ball position, let your weight shift to your left side—actually lean a bit toward your target. This is very important, because a bad chip will result if you move your weight to your left

A

The One-Lever Chip

The technique is the same as for the arms-and-shoulders putt, but the ball is played back in the stance and the weight is moved forward to produce a descending blow that gets the ball moderately airborne.

foot while slumping backward with your head and shoulders. When chipping, your eyes should not be above the backside of the ball; you should be looking down on the *target* side of the ball.

Picture a yardstick connecting your nose, breastbone, and navel when you stand up straight. It should still connect all three when you lean left for this shot.

All these maneuvers—the ball back in the stance, the hands forward, the weight forward, the body leaning left—promote a downward hit on the ball. This downward hit ensures crisp contact. A more shallow attack, as you might imagine, invites prior contact with the ground or grass, deadening the shot or throwing it off line.

The actual stroke is simplicity itself. Merely "putt" the ball with your arms-and-shoulders stroke, making certain that your body stays still and your wrists stay firm through impact. The ball will hop off the clubface and roll straight once it lands.

Remember, you don't have to "do" anything to get the ball airborne; the loft of the club will take care of that. The classic drill that makes this point is the golf-bag drill. Lay your golf bag down, just off the green and across your target line, so that you must hurdle it to get to the hole. From a few feet back, practice chipping over the bag to the hole with a pitching wedge or 9-iron. You

B

C

D

Practice chipping over a golf bag to cure any scooping tendencies. A firm downward blow with a lofted club will lift the ball sufficiently.

will quickly gain confidence in your ability to get chips airborne without resorting to scooping.

THE TWO-LEVER CHIP

This technique is analogous to the pop putt in that the hands and wrists are more active. Since hand action is desirable for this chip, you will want to use the conventional overlapping grip, not the reverse overlapping grip you use for putting.

The stance is the same as for the one-lever stroke: ball no farther forward than center, body leaning slightly left, hands ahead of ball and clubhead. The stroke is virtually the same, too, except that the wrists hinge slightly on the

A   B

The Two-Lever Chip
The hinging of the wrists is slight, but the hands feel much more active with this stroke.

takeaway and the right hand imparts a definite pop at impact. The important thing to remember is that the left hand has to remain firm through impact; you can't let your right hand roll over or overtake your left.

CONTROLLING DISTANCE

The success of most chips depends on how well one can control the distance the ball travels. Even a badly aimed chip will wind up fairly close to the hole if you get the distance right, but a 50-foot chip that rolls 70 feet is a turkey.

There are two schools of thought about distance control with the chipping clubs. One school holds that "feel" is paramount, and that feel is best developed by using the same club for all chips—say, an 8-iron. The one-club chipper takes a short backswing for short chips and a long swing for long chips.

The other school holds that feel is an elusive thing and that consistency is better achieved by hitting every chip with the same-length stroke. The multi-club chipper thus uses lofted clubs for short chips and less lofted clubs for long chips. The swing does not vary; the result does.

Both methods have their pros and cons. If you chip with just one club, you gradually develop the same feel for distance you have when tossing a ball underhand. You don't need to know precisely how far it is to the hole; you just chip it as hard as seems necessary, based on experience.

The downside is that you're stuck with one basic flight trajectory, making your one club patently wrong for certain chips. You may be the master of the 7-iron chip, but if you're in long grass 15 feet from the putting surface, you need more loft to carry the fringe. Similarly, a pitching wedge from 60 feet requires a pretty long backswing—always risky—and the ball may roll unpredictably upon landing. It's hardly a chip at all.

The beauty of the multi-club system is that every swing is the same; it's merely a matter of selecting the right club. The downside—the "beast" of it—is that you're less certain, until you have played lots of golf, how far the various clubs will fly the ball in the air and on what trajectory. This makes it hard to visualize shots into banks and slopes. It makes all chipping, for that matter, a pretty mechanical exercise . . . with bits of math thrown in for bad measure.

One-Club Distance Control

If you decide the one-club method is best for you, pick a club with enough loft to get the ball over greenside humps and long grass. An 8-iron or 9-iron will do the trick. (Your pro will be happy to sell you a "dedicated chipping iron" or chipper, which has a small heavy head and the loft of a 6- or 7-iron. The heavy head gets the ball in the air quickly, moves through long grass well, and helps you "feel the clubhead.")

Find a level practice green and hit a series of chips with different-length swings, pacing off how far the ball travels on average. For instance, your 9-iron chip with a 6-inch backswing may travel a mere 15 feet. With a 12-inch backswing, it may go 25 feet. Swing all the way back to 8 o'clock, and you may chip the ball 50 feet.

Once you know how far you hit your chips with swings of varying lengths, you can practice by shooting for tees stuck in the green at 5- or 10-foot intervals. When aiming for the 25-foot target, you'll learn to make the 6-inch backswing.

In time you won't have to "measure" your backswing; your feel will be automatic.

One-Swing Distance Control

If you decide on the one-swing technique, it's just a question of how long your standard stroke should be.

Short, preferably. Most good multi-club chippers swing the club back no farther than 7 o'clock.

Again, find a level practice green and pace off how far the ball travels when hit with different clubs. Here is a typical distance chart for a one-lever chip on greens of average speed:

Sand wedge	15 feet
Pitching wedge	25 feet
9-iron	35 feet
8-iron	45 feet
7-iron	55 feet
6-iron	65 feet
5-iron	75 feet

For in-between distances, simply shorten or lengthen your swing slightly or hit the ball a bit harder or softer. For example, a 30-foot chip might translate to a "hard" pitching wedge or a "soft" 9-iron.

During a round, you may occasionally have time to pace off the distance to the hole before you chip. Nothing beats knowing the distance. Otherwise, pace off chips when practicing until you get good at estimating distance by eye. If you know you have a 55-foot chip shot, and you also know you chip 55 feet with a 7-iron, then there's nothing left to do but aim and fire. Chipping uphill? Don't change your swing; take more club. For a 25-foot chip that's slightly uphill, pretend it's 35 feet and chip with your 9-iron. Steep hill? Use an 8-iron or a 7-iron.

Downhill, make similar adjustments. A normal 55-foot chip may call for a 7-iron, but if you're chipping downhill, downwind, and downgrain, you may be able to roll it that far with a pitching wedge.

Obviously greens that are unusually slow or fast will force you to refigure your club selection. But you *don't* have to adjust your swing. One-swing distance control ensures that you always stand over a chip shot with confidence.

THE CHIP FROM LONG GRASS

As often as not, we find ourselves chipping from greenside rough instead of close-clipped fringe grass. The basic arms-and-shoulders chipping stroke doesn't always work out of this shaggy stuff; grass gets between the blade and the ball, deadening contact and influencing spin.

Faced with such a shot, you have three choices. You can (1) use more of a body turn and pitch the ball at the flag with a lofted club; (2) switch from the one-lever to the two-lever chipping stroke; or (3) modify your one-lever setup.

Most pros use the two-lever stroke from long grass, but you should at least try the modified one-lever chip, popularized by Phil Rodgers a few years back.

The setup is almost exactly the same as for the regular one-lever chip. Use your putting grip again, but put the ball slightly farther back in your stance (toward your right foot). This encourages a more downward stroke. Your weight should be slightly over your left foot and your hands forward of the ball, off your left thigh. The big difference is that you stand closer to the ball and address it with the toe of the club down and the heel of the club raised off the ground. The shaft of the club should be practically vertical.

This may look and feel strange at first, but you will find that you can use your regular putting stroke from this setup. The club will not get tangled in the grass and ruin the shot. Just remember: no hand action. It's still an arms-and-shoulders stroke.

Ray Floyd uses this technique, and some pros consider him the best chipper in golf.

To chip from long grass using the one-lever technique, raise the heel of the club off the ground, play the ball well back in your stance, and stand closer to the ball. Remember to use the arms-and-shoulders stroke.

If you prefer to chip from long grass with the two-lever technique, few adjustments are necessary. Just move the ball a little farther back in your stance—to steepen the angle of attack and avoid as much grass as possible—and strike the ball more firmly.

Whichever method you employ, be wary when chipping out of deep grass against the grain. This lie smothers the club at impact and requires a much firmer stroke.

Recognize, too, that a ball chipped to land on the shorter fringe grasses will be affected by the grain. Greg Norman and Curtis Strange complained at a recent Masters at Augusta National because the fringes had been mowed in opposite directions. Said Norman, "If you don't land the ball in the right mower patch—which is what, twenty-two, twenty-four inches?—you're hosed. The ball will check up and won't go anywhere."

SIDEHILL CHIPS

On uneven lies, balance should always be your primary concern. If the ball is lower than your feet, set up with your feet somewhat farther apart and the ball center or back in your stance. Avoid leaning forward over the ball; you should feel as if you are sitting into the slope. If the slope is very steep, you may need to grip the club closer to the butt end to ensure crisp contact.

For chips with the ball higher than your feet, set up with your feet farther apart than normal, stand more upright than usual, and play the ball slightly

Sidehill Chips

When chipping with the ball lower than your feet, widen your stance and "sit into" the slope (left). When chipping with the ball higher than your feet, stand more upright and swing more around your body (right).

forward in your stance. From this lie, your normal swing could cause you to stub the toe of the club in the ground. To avoid this, swing more around your body, keeping the sole of the club parallel to the ground.

UPHILL AND DOWNHILL CHIPS

When chipping uphill, remember that the hill increases the effective loft of your club. To compensate, use one or two clubs more to cover the same distance—a 7-iron, say, instead of a 9-iron. Play the ball left of center in your stance and align your shoulders with the slope. This last point is key, because you want the clubface to meet the ball at the same angle it would on level ground. Failure to align the shoulders with the slope often results in a fat shot—that is, a shot in which the club hits the ground before it hits the ball.

On uphill chips, align your shoulders with the slope as shown (A) and use a less lofted club (B).

A

B

The downhill chip is the most difficult because the slope delofts the club, making the ball come off the hill low and hot. To compensate, use a more lofted club—a pitching wedge, say, instead of an 8-iron. Widen your stance for balance, and align your shoulders with the slope so the club will not contact the ground prematurely. (Note: don't expect your shoulders and the slope to be perfectly parallel. Your right hand is lower on the club than your left, keeping your right shoulder slightly below the left, even on level ground.)

Chipping downhill, the ball must be significantly back in your stance. On extremely steep hills, it's not unheard of to play the shot with the ball outside the right foot—that is, at ankle height or higher. To judge where you should play the ball, take one or two practice swings and see where your club brushes the grass.

On precipitous slopes, you may have to aim left and open the clubface to get the ball airborne.

On downhill chips, try to align your shoulders to the slope. They won't be quite parallel to the ground at address (B) because your right hand is lower than your left on the club.

A

B

The key to crisp downhill chips is to keep the club going down the slope on the follow-through. To do otherwise is to invite a skulled or topped shot, one that flies low or rolls along the ground.

CHIPPING TO SPOTS

The best chippers, at some point in their development, graduate from formula methods of distance control to pure touch. They also learn to focus on where they want the ball to land, rather than on the hole.

Usually this intermediate target is beyond the fringe and about 3 feet onto the putting surface. The idea is to get the ball on the ground and rolling as quickly as possible, while still leaving a margin for error.

A good drill is to chip the ball to the same spot with different clubs and observe how far the ball rolls after landing. With practice you should be able to visualize different versions of the same chip, making your choice according to how you read the green. For instance, you might want to take a more lofted club and chip over a hump or swale, thereby avoiding a double break. Or you might elect to keep the ball low and run it up to a pin on a green's upper level.

Obviously your ability to read for break and speed is as critical on chips as it is on putts. Just remember to start reading from the point where you expect the ball to land, not from where you're hitting.

THE PIN: IN OR OUT?

Any time you are off the putting surface, you have the option of leaving the flagstaff in the hole. That's what you should do: leave it in. Uphill chip, downhill, sidehill—it doesn't matter. You always have a better chance of sinking a chip with the pin in, and you'd be surprised how often a bound-for-trouble chip glances off the pin and stays near the hole.

Always in.

CHIPPING STRATEGY: CHARGE OR LAG?

If you learned your lessons on putting strategy, you know that most chipping situations call for a ball that dies near the hole—a lag. That's why most good players chip with the same mental picture they use for long putts—a 3-foot circle around the hole, a bucket, or whatever.

Many times, though, a chip is short or straight enough to charge like a putt. When that's the case, go for it. Picture the ball rolling into the center of the cup, and hit it hard enough to run a foot or so past the hole if you miss.

Strangely enough, the average player sinks more chip shots than long putts. It probably comes from not trying so hard.

9

Greenside Pitching

Phil Mickelson, who won his first PGA Tour event when he was still a college golfer at Arizona State University, has a unique approach to one of the hardest shots in golf: the downhill pitch over a sand bunker from a greenside mound.

Knowing there's no safe way to pop the ball onto the green from a conventional stance, Mickelson turns around, aims uphill and away from the flag, and sets his sand wedge wide open. From this unusual setup he takes a big smooth swing and lofts the ball backward over his head. As often as not, the ball lands softly and rolls close to the cup.

Mickelson's wrong-way lob illustrates an important point: to be a good greenside shotmaker you must be creative. The shots from 40 yards in require varied stances, different ball positions, and an ability to change trajectory at will. This is partly a matter of feel, but you will never develop feel unless you first understand and master the basic ball-striking principles.

Here are a few of those principles, as applied to greenside pitches:

- The farther forward you play the ball, the higher it wants to go.
- The more weight you put on your left side, the lower and farther the ball wants to go.
- The more you open your clubface, the higher the ball flies.

There are many more of these truisms, and no two golfers apply them exactly the same way. Pro A hits most of his pitch shots with the ball played off his left instep; he controls distance and trajectory by laying the clubface more or less open and varying his leg action. Pro B plays the same shot with the ball well back in his stance and virtually no hand action. Some pros teach that the pitch shot is "all right-hand," but touring pros of the 1930s and '40s

93

Greenside shotmaking, no matter what the lie of the ball, requires creativity and, sometimes, nerve.

hit feather-soft pitches by playing the ball back, opening the clubface, and dropping the clubhead on the ball with a steep left-handed stroke.

These differences should not surprise us, because the pitch shot employs more body turn than the chip, making it more or less a full swing. And how many ways of swinging a golf club are there? A thousand? Some of us swing on a very upright plane, some of us swing more around our bodies. Some of us manipulate the clubface with our hands and wrists, some of us square the blade with little or no hand action. Some of us hit the ball from inside the target path (hookers), and some of us cut across the ball from the outside (slicers).

Without knowing how *you* swing, it's a challenge to give hard-and-fast rules for pitching and sand play. If the following techniques don't work for you, it's probably because your setup and full-swing mechanics differ significantly from those of the pro in the photographs.

Don't despair. Phil Mickelson didn't learn to hit golf balls backward by copying Arnold Palmer. He creatively applied his knowledge of the ball-striking principles and played around with the shot until he found a setup and swing that worked. You can do the same thing. Your misses will tell you what you're doing wrong. Just experiment with your setup and swing until you find the right combination for you.

THE PITCH-AND-RUN

If you polled the touring professionals, most of them would tell you that, around the green, low is better than high. That is, most good players try to get the ball on the green and rolling at the flag as quickly as possible. If they can roll it there with a putter, they putt. If they can't putt, they chip. And if they can't chip, they look first to the pitch-and-run shot.

The pitch-and-run is a shot that lands partway and then rolls the rest of the way to the hole. How far (and how high) you fly the ball depends on how much terrain you have to carry. If your entrance to the green is relatively flat and unguarded, you can pitch the ball to the fringe with a middle iron and let the ball roll the rest of the way like a putt. But if the green is elevated and surrounded by deep rough, you might take a more lofted club and fly the ball close to the pin.

The chart below gives a typical flight-to-roll ratio for various irons, assuming the blade is square at impact:

5-iron	1/4 flight	3/4 roll
7-iron	1/3 flight	2/3 roll
9-iron	1/2 flight	1/2 roll
Pitching wedge	2/3 flight	1/3 roll
Sand wedge	3/4 flight	1/4 roll

You select your club by estimating how far you are from the flag and how much of that distance you must carry to land safely on the green. For instance, if you have 80 feet to the flag but only 30 feet to the edge of the putting surface, you'll probably want to land the ball 10 feet or so onto the green—halfway to the flag in this example. The club for a shot that is half carry and half roll is the 9-iron, so you'll take your 9-iron and try to land the ball precisely on the spot you've selected, 10 feet beyond the fringe. If you succeed in hitting that spot, the ball should roll the remaining 40 feet to the flag.

A good drill is to hit various clubs to an intermediate target and watch what happens. In the above example, a perfectly hit 5-iron will scoot way past the hole, but an equally well struck sand wedge will stop 27 feet short of the hole.

To hit the pitch-and-run shot, choke down 2 or 3 inches on the club and address the ball with a stance that is slightly narrower than usual. Play the ball in the middle of your stance (even with your sternum), and balance your weight evenly between your feet. This "vanilla" setup encourages a not-so-steep swing path and a medium-high trajectory.

The swing is a simple turn away from the ball and a turn back. The arms go back to at least 8 o'clock—considerably longer on full pitches with lofted clubs—and work through the ball to a finishing position at least as high as the backswing. How much you hinge your wrists depends on your full-swing philosophy, but the overall feel should be soft, particularly on short pitches: soft grip pressure, smooth acceleration through the ball, a follow-through with no recoil or loss of balance. You want to contact the ball first and the turf second, but don't confuse this shot with the chip, which calls for a sharp downward hit on the ball and no follow-through.

If you can't hit the ball short distances with your wedges—that is, if you fly the ball over the green no matter how easy you try to swing—you are probably swinging too much with your arms. To slow down the clubhead, turn your arms and body more as a unit and don't let your arms rush ahead on the downswing.

A   B   C

The bump-and-run is the pitch-and-run shot played into a greenside bank. Don't attempt this shot into thick Bermuda rough; the ball will probably be smothered on the second bounce.

THE LOB

Sometimes you have no choice: you have to hit it high. You face a short shot over a sand bunker, or a pitch over a creek, or a shot to a tight pin position on a terraced green. In these situations you can't putt it, chip it, or bounce it to the hole with the pitch-and-run. You need to fly the ball high and make it drop softly near the flag with little or no roll.

To pull this shot off you need to review the ball-striking principles mentioned above. Any of the following actions make the ball fly higher:

- Using a more lofted club
- Playing the ball more forward in the stance
- Opening the clubface to create more loft
- Putting more weight on your right side
- Addressing the ball with your hands behind the clubhead, not ahead

Applied all at the same time, these measures allow you to slide the clubface under the ball and pop it skyward.

For most golfers, the club of choice is obvious: the sand wedge. Even

D

E

better is the increasingly popular 60- to 65-degree lob wedge, also known as the "third wedge." This specialty club has enough loft to hit the ball into your own pocket, but it has a shallower flange than a sand wedge, to minimize bounce. This comes in handy when you're trying to slide the club under the ball from a close fairway lie.

Just how open you set the clubface at address depends on how high you want to hit the ball. To drop it down a chimney, a pro will open the clubface till the flange is flat on the ground and the face points at the sky.

The more you open the clubface, the more you must compensate by aligning your body and swing path left of the target. The reason for this is apparent if you consider what would happen if you took a square stance and hit the ball with an open clubface—you'd hit a pop-up to right field. That's what the lob shot is: a pop-up to right.

To set up properly, grip the club and pre-set the loft by soling the club on the ground. Do this *before* you go through your pre-shot routine.

Next, place the clubface behind the ball so that the leading edge is square to the direction you want to go. A good practice aid is a tee placed upside down on the clubface. The tee will predict the ball's initial launch direction and trajectory.

A tee on the clubface predicts the direction and trajectory the ball will take when lobbed.

Finally, align your body to the ball, ignoring the clubface. Your feet, hips, and shoulders should be aligned well left of the target, and the ball should be even with or slightly forward of your sternum. Your weight should also be more toward your right side than usual.

From this setup, you need only swing smoothly along your body line—*not* toward the target—and the ball should go up like a Roman candle.

The lob leaves no divot, so check the ground for evidence. On fairway grass, the only sign that you've been there should be a bruise or roughed-up spot. If you find yourself taking a divot, go back to the ball-striking principles and see which one you're violating.

Wristiness is not required to lob the ball, and on short pitches you can strike the ball with very little hinging. However, there's a practical limit to how far you can lob the ball without using your wrists. Practice with varying degrees of hand action to see how high and how far the ball goes.

It *is* essential that the clubhead come through low to the ground and open. Don't let your right hand roll over and release until well after impact. Put another way, the back of your left hand should still be pointing skyward on the follow-through.

One of the pitfalls of the lob is that it's so much fun to hit. Keep in mind that it is the least accurate of the greenside shots. If you can chip the ball to the hole or pitch it close with a less lofted club, do so. Similarly, resist the temptation to hit it off a tight lie or hardpan. The ball needs to be sitting up for you to slide your club under it.

The lob from hardpan is rarely a pop-up to right. More often, it is a line drive to center.

THE PITCH FROM LONG GRASS

When your ball is sitting up in long grass, you must protect against sliding the entire clubhead under the ball, sending it nowhere. To guard against this mishap, play the ball farther back in your stance, position your hands more forward, square up the blade, shift your weight left, and make sure you hit the ball before the ground. In other words, don't lob it unless you're sure you can get the middle of the clubface on the ball.

If your ball is sitting down in greenside rough, you need to play a shot similar to the explosion shot from sand. Take your sand wedge, open up the clubface, play the ball forward in your stance, and set your weight to the left. This shot requires pronounced hand action. By hinging your wrists abruptly, you create the steep angle of attack necessary to explode the ball out of the grass.

On short pitches from long grass use this same setup, but pick the club up abruptly and just drop it on the ball. Sounds dangerous, but the ball pops out cleanly and trickles only a few feet upon landing. Don't expect too much, though; even the pros can't predict what this shot will do.

To pitch a ball buried in greenside rough, open the clubface and hinge your wrists abruptly on the backswing. Hitting down sharply behind the ball makes it come out like an explosion shot from sand (see page 103).

10

Bunker Play

Toby Lyons is an old golf pro, a gruff character with a big-featured leathery face and thin gray hair raked straight back over his skull. He played in fifteen U.S. Opens in the 1940s and early '50s, and the names of contemporaries fall easily from his lips: Sarazen, Snead, Nelson. In recent years he has spent his summers teaching at the Niagara Falls (N.Y.) Country Club, but I met him a couple of years ago in a greenside bunker in Sun City, Florida.

"It's the easiest shot in golf, boys," Toby said to my golf school class. He dropped a ball in the sand, dug in with his feet, and splashed the ball out with a swing no longer than a summer sausage. The ball stopped a foot from the pin.

He threw down another ball. "Don't open the blade. Just hit behind the ball." He chipped out another; it slid a foot past the pin. He threw down another ball, stepped on it, kicked some sand over it. "Fried-egg lie. Gotta close the clubface." He planted his feet, swung, and the ball stopped 2 feet from the hole. "That's all there is to it, boys. Go to work."

A minute later, sand was flying, grown men were grunting, and Toby's three balls still sat in isolated splendor near the hole.

"No, no, no!" he roared. I looked up. He was staring at me with an anguished expression on his face. "Not like *that*. Like *this!*" He made an abbreviated flick with the club. I tried to imitate his swing and left the ball in the trap again.

"No, no, no," he said—softly this time. He grabbed the shaft of my sand wedge and yanked it back and through while I held the grip. "Do *this*." Instead, I did something else.

"No," he shouted. "Can't you do this?"

"Apparently not," I said.

"Your swing is too big," he muttered. He moved on.

Hitting well from bunkers requires precise technique.

A minute later, I heard him scolding a retired pilot whose sole claim to self-esteem was that he had once been entrusted with 800 tons of Boeing 707 and the life of the President of the United States. "You're doing *this* . . . I'm doing *this!*" Pause. Sound of sand splashing and ball landing softly on green.

"Why can't you do what I do?"

That, of course, was the question we had paid $1,540 to have answered.

Most tournament players are like Toby: baffled by the average player's fear of sand. For touring pros, the explosion shot *is* an easy shot. Good sand players get up and down from bunkers 70 percent of the time from distances most of us would need three putts to solve. When trying to reach par 5s in 2, the pros would rather plunk the ball in a bunker than roll it into a grassy swale. The ball is easier to control out of sand, they say. The margin for error is greater.

What the good players often overlook is that they have one big advantage over the weekend golfer: a place to practice. Our fear of sand is often simply fear of the unknown.

The material in this chapter assumes that you have access to a practice bunker and can spend, say, thirty uninterrupted minutes hitting balls out of it. If you can't—well, don't be too hard on yourself when your sand game remains less than perfect.

THE SAND WEDGE

It helps to know how the sand wedge works. If you examine a sand wedge and a pitching wedge side by side, you will see that the clubheads are fundamentally different. The pitching wedge, when soled, presents a sharp leading edge that sits right on the ground. Swing downward with this club and the leading edge digs into the turf or sand after contact with the ball.

The leading edge of the sand wedge, in contrast, sits atop a broad flange. This blunt flange, if used properly, prevents the clubhead from cutting deep into the ground. In golf parlance, the bigger the flange, the bigger the "bounce."

Think of the sand wedge as a Swiss Army knife with only two functions. The leading edge is the "digger." The more you close the clubface, shift your weight to the left, or move the ball back in your stance, the deeper the leading edge will dig into the sand.

The flange is the "bouncer." The more you open the face, shift your weight to the right, or play the ball forward in your stance, the less the club will dig

The flange on a sand wedge (left) keeps the club from digging deep into the sand. The bigger the flange, the more bounce. When soled, a pitching wedge (right) presents a sharper leading edge than a sand wedge's.

into the sand. The flange actually functions like an airplane's wing, providing lift to force the clubhead up and out of the sand.

This is important, because the object in sand play is not to hit the ball itself, but rather to throw the sand *under* the ball up on the green. The ball simply rides this cushion of sand to safety.

To recap: The leading edge digs. The flange bounces.

THE EXPLOSION SHOT

The stance for the explosion shot from sand is a bit wider than that for the pitch shot. The ball is played slightly forward of center and your weight should be carried evenly over both feet. For balance, and to help get the clubhead under the ball, you should work your feet an inch or two down into the sand. But remember, there is a two-stroke penalty for grounding a club in a hazard. Make sure you don't touch the sand with the clubhead before you swing.

If you have watched much golf, you know that most good players execute the explosion shot with an open stance and a wide-open clubface. They do this to spin the ball, which increases their control. It is a misconception, however,

When practicing your bunker shots, draw a line in the sand behind the ball to use as a target.

that an open stance and clubface are required to escape sand. There is sufficient bounce built into the modern sand wedge to get the ball out even if you set your body and clubface square to the target line. Just make certain that you play the ball forward of center so the leading edge of the club won't dig too deeply into the sand.

How far behind the ball should you hit the sand? That's a matter of argument. Some good players say to take an inch or two of sand. Others say you can hit as far as 6 inches behind the ball and still put the ball near the hole.

The dispute probably has little to do with differences in technique and more to do with imprecise measurement. As an experiment, draw a line in the sand and take a stance straddling it. Then try to hit the line with the leading edge of your sand wedge. Surprise! The impact crater will probably start 2 or 3 inches behind the line.

Now lay the clubface wide open and take another swing at the line. This time, the crater will start as much as 6 inches behind the line.

Confusing? You bet. The divot taken out of the sand doesn't tell you where the club entered the sand; it tells you where the most rearward part of the flange hit the sand.

Some good players tackle this problem by imagining that the clubface is transparent. They pretend they can see the flange on the bottom of the club. Then, instead of aiming the edge of the clubface at a point in the sand, they try to hit that point with the front of the flange.

Others argue that it isn't necessary to be precise about the distance because the margin for safety is so great. If you set up correctly and take a normal swing along your body line, the club will hit the sand in the right place. The key isn't *where* you hit the sand; it's whether the angle of attack is correct.

Toby Lyons notwithstanding, the modern sand swing is a long swing, even on short bunker shots. Without sufficient clubhead speed, the club won't make it through the sand unless you hit very close to the ball. Hitting close to the ball increases the risk that you'll hit it before you hit the sand, causing it to rocket across the green.

It is also important to pick the club up quickly by hinging the wrists abruptly on the backswing. This creates a very steep swing plane. If your clubhead hits the sand at an angle that is too shallow, the clubhead won't dig in at all, but will skid off the sand, "bellying" the ball (hitting a line drive). The steeper the angle of attack, the higher the ball will fly and the softer it will land.

The swing should be smooth and unhurried, with careful attention paid to a high finish on the follow-through. Failure to swing through the ball is one of the prime culprits in botched sand play.

As on the lob shot, you must also make certain that your right hand does not roll over your left until well after impact. Closing the clubface too early will make it dig into the sand, smothering the shot; at best, the ball will come out low and hard. The clubface should face the sky on the follow-through.

When executed properly, the explosion shot leaves a long shallow crater in the sand. If your divots are deep and short, and if you have trouble swinging to a high finish, your downswing is too steep. (Another symptom: your ball rarely gets out of the trap.) Check your setup to make sure the ball is forward of center. Be certain that your weight isn't too much on your left side. And check to make sure your right shoulder is a little lower than your left at address.

A

B

C

The Explosion Shot

The clubface never touches the ball, only the sand. Start by digging your feet into the sand until the spikes take a good hold; you cannot afford any slippage while in a bunker. Your feet are now slightly below the level of the ball, so shorten up on the club just a bit. At address, set up so the ball is off your left heel and your hands are well forward, opposite

G

H

I

D E F

your left leg. The length of the backswing is governed in part by the distance between the ball and the target. Strike the club into the sand approximately one full ball diameter behind the ball (but experiment to find the distance that suits you), and don't baby the swing. As you hit the ball, keep your right hand under your left and continue to a high finish. Don't quit on a bunker shot, or you will probably get the chance to try another explosion shot with your next swing.

J K

The clubface must still be open and pointing at the sky at this stage of the follow-through. Don't let your right hand cross over your left.

The Explosion Shot
from an Open Stance

As mentioned above, most good players play this shot with an open stance and an open blade for added control. And not just a little open; you can open the clubface so wide that it seems to point straight up. This setup frightens high-handicappers because it looks as though the ball might hit the hosel. Actually the open stance prevents this from happening, and the flange slides through the sand like a rudder through water.

When playing the explosion with an open clubface, you do have to open your stance slightly, but not as much as you might think. Because the ball rides out on a cushion of sand, it tends to follow the direction of the swing more than the direction of the clubface. Just align your feet and hips slightly left of your target and swing along your body line.

If you hit the sand at least 2 inches behind the ball, you'll get a nice soft shot that lands with little spin and trickles a few feet before stopping. If you're brave, you can try hitting the sand a half inch or an inch behind the ball. You'll get impressive backspin and sidespin, causing the ball to check up or dance a few feet to the right. But beware: if you catch the ball before the sand, you'll wish you hadn't.

Controlling Distance from Sand

There are two ways to control how far you hit the explosion shot. You can (1) keep the distance you hit behind the ball constant and change the length and force of your swing, or (2) keep the force of your swing constant and take more or less sand.

There is no consensus among good players as to which method is better. Most amateurs will probably find it easier to keep their setups constant and vary the force of the swing.

If you prefer the second method, just remember: the closer you hit behind the ball, the farther it will fly. Always make the same swing, no matter how far it is to the pin.

(The more-or-less-sand technique is almost mandatory on very short explosion shots. If you have 10 feet or less to carry, play the ball a little more forward in your stance, open the clubface a little more, and take a normal aggressive swing at the ball. The extra sand you take will deaden the impact and produce a soft knuckleball of a shot.)

LONG BUNKER SHOTS

This shot bothers even the best players. From 30 or 40 yards off the green, the explosion shot is fraught with peril. Take too much sand and you may not get out of the bunker. Hit the ball cleanly and you may fly it over the green.

Australia's Greg Norman plays the long bunker shot like a standard explosion shot, but he gets additional distance by using his full quiver of short irons, 7-iron through pitching wedge. The shortcoming of this approach is that none of these clubs have flanges, so Norman has to hit very close behind the ball. If you think you're as precise a ball striker as Greg Norman, read no farther.

The rest of us will stick with the sand wedge. To get more distance with the explosion shot, you need to make a few adjustments: (1) Square up your stance so you're only slightly open at most. (2) Square the clubface at address. (3) Hit the sand closer to the ball—say, an inch behind. And (4) take your normal full swing, not the more upright swing you use for the greenside explosion shot. These adustments will produce a lower trajectory, more carry, and more roll.

Don't expect miracles, though. If you get your ball on the green and within two-putt range, you're doing fine.

The Long Bunker Shot

To execute the difficult long bunker shot,
square your stance, square the clubface, and
hit closer behind the ball. Take your normal
full swing, not the steep, wristy swing used for
the standard explosion shot.

A

D

E

B

C

F

G

BURIED LIES

Most of the time the ball sits up nicely on sand. But if the sand is soft, the ball may end up partially or totally buried.

The kinder of these situations is the "fried-egg lie," so called because the ball, in its impact crater, looks like an egg sunny-side up.

No major adjustment is necessary for this shot. Just visualize the clubhead sliding under the entire egg and throw the whole thing up on the green, egg white and all. If the crater is unusually wide or deep, close the face of your sand wedge at address and hit down a little harder behind the ball. But remember to follow through.

The buried lie, with only the top of the ball showing in the sand, calls for a little more force and a little ingenuity. Whatever you do, don't try to hit this shot with an open clubface—the flange won't let you get deep enough to slide under the ball. Instead, aim a little right and "shut down" the clubface—close it so the leading edge is pointing left of the target and the face is perpendicular to the ground. Play the ball back in your stance and let your weight shift a little to your left foot. Then pick the club straight up and slam it steeply down right behind the ball. Don't follow through—just drive the clubhead into the ground, hard. You won't be able to fly the ball very far with so much sand between the clubface and the ball, but the ball will come out running. Allow for plenty of roll.

Some players don't use the sand wedge when the ball is buried. They hit a standard explosion shot with a 9-iron or pitching wedge, counting on the unflanged sole to cut deep enough into the sand.

The fried-egg lie.
The deeper the ball is buried, the more you must close the clubface to dig under it at impact.

UNEVEN LIES

Sand shots from slopes require the usual adjustments at address. For the uphill explosion shot, take a firm wide stance with most of your weight on your lower foot. Align your shoulders with the slope and open the clubface. Then take a healthy cut, being careful to drive the clubhead into the sand under the ball.

Another common technique for uphill shots works if your ball is buried in a steep bunker face. Instead of opening the clubface, hood it—that is, aim the clubface left of your swing path. Instead of aligning yourself with the slope, stand up straight with most of your weight on your right leg. Just hit hard underneath the ball and watch it pop out like magic.

The downhill sand shot is more difficult because the slope makes the ball come out on a low trajectory. Set up with the ball farther back in your stance and your weight on your left foot. (Your right leg should be flexed against the hill, but no more than is required for balance.) As usual with hill shots, try to align your shoulders with the slope.

From this setup, the swing path will be extremely steep, but you still want a smooth swing and as full a follow-through as possible, given the situation. Accept that the ball will come out lower than normal.

Hood the clubface if your ball is buried in the steep face of a bunker. Hit hard beneath the ball and it should pop right out.

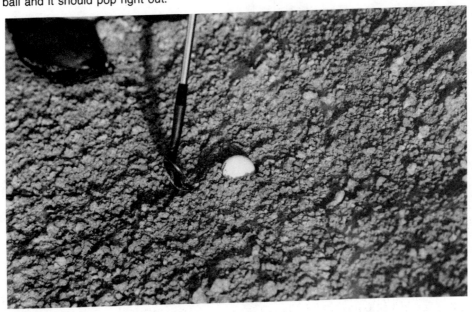

The downhill bunker shot calls for an abrupt lifting of the club on the backswing. Be sure to follow through down the slope. Otherwise, you'll blade the ball.

WET SAND

Wet sand isn't sand; it's mud. Your sand wedge, therefore, is dangerous—the flange will bounce off the firm surface and belly your ball to kingdom come.

To explode from wet sand, simply substitute your pitching wedge or a lob wedge for the sand wedge and play it as you would a normal explosion shot. The sharper leading edge of either of these clubs will cut through the mud and get you safely on the green.

DYE-ABOLICAL BUNKERS

Should you ever have the good fortune to play golf in Scotland, you will eventually find yourself up to your ears in a greenside pot bunker. From these deep shell craters (and from steep-faced trench-style bunkers) there is often no way to play a shot to the hole. You simply take your medicine by turning around and playing a shot backwards to the fairway.

American golf course architect Pete Dye visited Scotland early in his career, and he liked what he saw. His best-known courses (Harbour Town Links, TPC at Sawgrass, PGA West Stadium Course) call for demanding shots from pot bunkers and deep grass-walled greenside bunkers. These hazards are particularly difficult because Dye builds them deep with flat bottoms. The sand is usually light-grained but shallow—the hard bunker floor is an inch or so below the sand.

Should you attempt this shot with a square clubface or with the ball played back in your stance, be ready to throw your arms up to protect your face. The flange will skip right off that hard floor and rocket the ball into the grass wall.

To escape Dye's dungeon, you need to make a very shallow cut with your wedge, and that cut must begin closer to the ball than usual. Play the shot with an open stance, an open clubface, and with the ball forward in your stance. Cock your hands very quickly on the takeaway (to create a steep angle of attack), and "spank" the sand right behind the ball.

If the hole is cut close behind the grass wall, you need a shot that comes out soft with little roll: take a slower, more measured swing. If you need more distance, swing faster and harder. Dye's bunkers make it risky to try to control distance by taking more or less sand.

BUNKER STRATEGY: WHEN TO PLAY SAFE

The primary consideration in sand play is always to *get out*. Too many amateurs try to play shots they aren't capable of playing, often because they lack imagination. You don't have to aim at the flag, you know. If you're in a deep greenside bunker with 30 feet of sand and a steep grassy bank to carry to a tight pin location—there's a pond behind the flag, say—consider an alternative route. Sometimes it makes sense to come out of a trap sideways—to shorten the carry, for example, or to enlarge the target. A putt of any length is preferable to a second shot from sand.

Remember, too, that the ball will do its thing once it lands. Drop the ball on the high side and let it run down to the hole, if you can. Or play it below the hole and leave yourself an easier uphill putt.

You don't have to let your brain take a vacation just because *you're* on the beach.

Afterword

Play alone and practice with friends.

No, this last piece of advice is not backwards. Most self-improvement programs fail because they follow the old "woodshed" model. (That's what old-time jazz musicians called it when they went off in private to work on their chops—"goin' to the woodshed.") In golf, Ben Hogan was the ultimate woodshedder. A driven perfectionist, he hit hundreds, thousands, of practice balls a week. He had room for little but golf in his life, and it showed.

A more recent example: Nick Faldo.

Woodshedding works for the pros because they are totally committed to the game. They have unlimited time and energy for golf. It *doesn't* work for us. Golf is our avocation, not our vocation.

Nevertheless, the pictures and lessons in this book probably have you in a woodshedding frame of mind. You're thinking, "I'm going to practice two hours a day for the next hundred days, and when I'm done the guys in my foursome won't believe my new short game!"

Hey, if it were that easy we'd all be able to play the saxophone, dance like Fred Astaire, paint watercolors, and speak several languages fluently.

Here's a more likely scenario: You'll practice two hours a day for three days, and you'll get blisters. You'll see immediate improvement on chip shots and get all excited—only to wonder why you're suddenly hitting them fat on day three. You'll master the lob shot, but then you won't be able to hit the standard pitch.

By the second week, you'll be practicing for an hour every third day. You'll quickly get bored with the circle drill—with *all* the putting drills, for that matter—and you'll spend less and less time on the putting green.

Come Saturday morning, when you're actually out on the course, your

117

Ben Hogan was the ultimate woodshedder, but you're not Ben Hogan. Better to practice your short game with friends than to sequester yourself unnecessarily.

mind will go totally blank. You'll get caught up in the small talk and banter of a normal round, lose your concentration, and hack your way through eighteen holes of hell.

By week three, you'll have put this book on the shelf and given up all hope of lowering your golf score—until a new book or video comes along promising "ten strokes off your handicap in thirty days."

It's the classic pattern. It's what awaits you if you start a practice program based on the work habits of the pros.

PLAY ALONE

Until your new short-game skills have become second nature, the techniques outlined in these pages will demand your total concentration. You won't be able to chat with your cart mate, monitor your bets, or practice normal golf etiquette. That's one good argument for playing solo for a while.

Here's another: you will play *slower*. (All that thinking takes time.)

And yet another: your new skills won't hold up under the pressure of being watched.

Granted, it isn't easy to golf alone these days, particularly if you live in certain big cities. But most golf courses have slow times or slow seasons. The hours just after dawn and before sunset are wonderful times to play, and many courses are deserted then. Foggy, misty days in March? That's what it's like in Scotland and Ireland most of the time, and it rarely gets in the way of golf there.

Playing alone, you can keep your mind on business—or rather, on play. And you can hit extra shots. Practicing on a golf course is generally forbidden, but most clubs wink at the solo golfer who plays two balls. Missed that easy pitch over the bunker? Play it again from the same spot. Spied a nice mound behind the green? Try that downhill chip you've been working on.

Real golf situations are found on the golf course, not on the range.

PRACTICE WITH FRIENDS

Drills are boring, and you'll never match the zeal of Curtis Strange, who works on his putting stroke by making literally hundreds of 2-foot putts in a single practice session.

Why feel guilty? Curtis does it because it's his job and he gets rich from it. You do it, and you just wind up a very dull person.

Practice *is* important. The mystery is why everyone thinks it should be done in private. After all, it's not shameful to practice, and there's no virtue in boredom. Practice can even be fun, if shared with a friend. For instance:

- Play H-O-R-S-E with someone. That's right, the old basketball shooting game, only with golf clubs. If you have a practice green with a flag, fine, but any target will do. Player A calls his shot: "Lob wedge to within 10 feet." If he pulls the shot off, player B has to match the shot or take a letter, starting with H. If player A misses, player B calls the shot, and so on. The first player to get all five letters in "horse" loses.
- "Request." Practice pitching with a friend, but each of you gets to call the other's shot. "Lob one over that bunker to the yellow flag." "Hit a low pitch-and-run to the 50-yard sign." "Pitch it onto the cage of the tractor picking up balls."
- "Putt for dough." Play eighteen holes on the putting clock with a buddy or your spouse at a quarter a hole. Fifty cents for aces. Or get several players on the putting green and play "skins." (Quarter a hole, but only if one player wins the hole outright. Ties don't count.)

Games like these take the drudgery out of practice. They also make you less self-conscious about your game, because you get used to hitting both good and bad shots with someone watching. (The woodshed approach—practicing away from prying eyes—creates tremendous performance anxiety when you finally tee it up in public.)

Plus, you get useful feedback. Tournament players constantly ask each other for help with their setup and swing plane, so why shouldn't you? You can ask: "Are my hips square? Are my eyes over the ball? Is the ball about an inch forward in my stance? Is the clubface aimed where I think it is, at the right edge of the hole?"

Coaching you *don't* need (except from a pro), but another pair of eyes is invaluable in golf.

AND FINALLY . . . "FEEL"

Ultimately you will develop feel, or touch. Somewhere down the road—two months from now, two years from now, twenty thousand putts from now—your putting stroke will become less mechanical and more instinctive. Your

Once you develop a feel for your putts, your score—as well as your mood around the pin—should improve considerably.

chips and pitches will be tension-free. You will be able to visualize shot options *and* execute them.

"When I play my best golf, I feel as if I'm in a fog," the great Mickey Wright once said, "standing back watching the earth in orbit with a golf club in my hands."

That's what feel is like—a sublime mindlessness that lets you concentrate on your target, and not on swing thoughts or images from a book.

Don't be shocked if your touch never quite reaches the standard of a Mickey Wright or a Ben Crenshaw. The great tournament players are great partly because they bring unusual hand-eye coordination to the game. If you are older than, say, fifteen, you probably don't have similar gifts in your sports attic.

You *should* see marked improvement, though, if you follow the advice in this book. Two areas in particular are almost instant stroke-savers: chipping and distance control with the putter. You would do well to drill on those two the most, emphasizing the one-swing multi-club approach in chipping and the "one foot equals one inch" formula in putting. Pitching and sand play will take longer to master, and you should expect setbacks and some frustration.

Remember, you don't have to be young, big, strong, or even wise to putt well. You simply have to learn the fundamentals and practice them. You'll know you've turned the corner when somebody says, "I knew you when you were the world's worst putter."

That's another kind of feel—feeling good about your game.

Glossary

A

Arms-and-shoulders putting. A style of putting characterized by unified movement of the arms and shoulders, but with no movement of the wrists.

B

Bent. A finely textured species of grass used for putting greens; it is especially prevalent on cooler-weather courses.

Bermuda. A coarsely textured species of grass in which the strands intertwine. Used for both fairways and putting greens, especially in hot, humid climates.

Blade putter. A putter whose shaft meets one end of the clubhead.

Break. The lateral direction in which a putt rolls, resulting from a green's contour. Often used with "left to right" or "right to left," as in "That putt's going to break left to right." Reading a putt's break and compensating for it in an actual putt are two of the more significant skills any golfer should develop.

Bunker. A sand hazard along a fairway or near a green.

Bump-and-run. A pitch-and-run shot played into a greenside bank. *See* Pitch-and-run.

C

Center-shafted putter. A putter whose blade extends in both directions from the end of the shaft.

Charge. To putt a ball with enough velocity that it will reach the hole—or roll far beyond it if the putt is off-target. *See* Lag.

Chip. A greenside shot similar to a putt, but with the ball played back in the stance and the weight moved forward to produce a descending blow and a slightly lofted ball trajectory.

Claw. A grip style employed by some golfers using the long-shafted putter, so named because the position of the golfer's index and middle fingers resembles a bird's foot structure.

Cross-hand grip. A putting grip in which the upper and lower hands switch positions from the normal golf grip.

F

Flange-blade putter. The basic straight-blade putter with a somewhat massive extension added to the back of the clubhead.

Fringe. Or *collar:* the strip of medium-length grass that surrounds a green.

Fried-egg lie. A ball lying partially buried in sand, so named because it resembles a fried egg over easy.

H

Hazard. An area, such as a bunker or a pond, in which the privileges of play are restricted.

Hood. To position a club's face downward, toward the ground; a technique used when trying to pop a ball from the steep face of a bunker.

Hosel. The socket into which the shaft of an iron is fitted.

I

Investment casting. A process for manufacturing golf irons wherein molten metal is poured into preformed molds that have the scoring lines and the stampings contained in them; as compared to *forging,* where a raw head is individually hand-filed and ground into a finished product by a skilled craftsman.

L

Lag. To hit a long putt with just enough speed for the ball to reach the hole or to stop within a 3-foot radius of it.

M

Mallet-head putter. A putter whose shaft joins near the end of the clubhead at a steep angle, and whose head is heavy and shaped like a half moon.

N

Neutral grip. A quality that characterizes most good putting grips, wherein neither hand dominates the other, and each grips the putter firmly enough to maintain control but not so tightly as to induce tension.

O

One-lever chip. A form of chipping that employs the arms-and-shoulders putting style.

Overlapping grip. A standard golf grip wherein the little finger of the bottom hand interlocks with the index finger of the top hand.

P

Pitch. A golf shot that lobs or lofts the ball into the air, used for short approaches to the green.

Pitch-and-run. A shot so played that part of the desired distance is covered by the roll of the ball after it strikes the ground.

Plumb bobbing. A technique for reading the break of a putt by sighting the ball and hole down the length of a putter suspended vertically at eye level.

Pop putter. A golfer who putts with active hands. *See* Stroke putter.

Pop putting. A type of putting in which the wrists are "active" and the putter's follow-through is usually short and decisive.

R

Reverse overlapping grip. The standard grip used in putting, wherein the index finger of the upper hand overlaps one or more knuckles of the lower hand.

Rough. The part of the course that is not tee, fairway, green, fringe, or hazard.

S

Sole. To hold a golf club in such a way that the entire length of the head touches the ground. A good putter should sole naturally when the golfer assumes the putting stance.

Straight-blade putter. A putter with a thin, lightweight clubhead, useful for putting on fast greens.

Stroke putter. A golfer who putts with "passive" hands. *See* Pop putter.

T

Texas wedge. A putter used to play a ball out of a sand trap when a putt is the safest and easiest way to get the ball on the green.

Two-lever chip. A chip in which the second lever is formed by the wrists, which break slightly during the swing.

Wrist putting. *See* Pop putting. A type of putting in which the wrists are active.

Y

Yips. A common greenside affliction suffered by golfers and characterized by inexplicable jerks and tremors during short putts. Cures include meditation, hypnosis, prayer, abstinence, finding a new sport, or—less bothersome—minimizing the action of the hands. In other words: stroke it, don't pop it.